OPEN YOUR EYES

DISCOVER WHO YOU ARE IN THE REALM OF THE SPIRIT

Authors

Vasyl Pechko   Vince Baker

Scripture quotations are taken from the Holy Bible, King James Version (KJV), and Amplified Bible, Classic Edition (AMPC). The King James Version is in the public domain in the United States of America. All bolding and emphasis are added by the author.

Editors: Eunice Baker & Cherryl Rodney

Printed in the United States of America

TABLE OF CONTENTS

Dedication

We dedicate this book to our faithful Heavenly Father, Jesus our Lord, and the precious Holy Spirit. Our hearts are thankful for all you have done, and what you plan to do in the next phase of our lives.

We also dedicate this book to our loving and supportive wives, Elina and Eunice. The Lord knows the faithfulness you show God, your family, and the Church of God.

Finally, we dedicate this book to our loving family and friends who stand by us as we serve our Lord.

God Bless You All!

FORWARD

I have been privileged to know Vasyl Pechko and Vince Baker. Their unwavering faith and deep commitment to sharing the Gospel are evident in all they do. They have invested countless hours studying the Bible, seeking to understand and share its profound truths. Their insights into the transformative power of the "New Man" are truly inspiring.

In this book, Vasyl and Vince emphasize the importance of opening one's spiritual eyes to perceive the unseen *Realm of the Spirit*. They explore the core teachings of Jesus Christ, explaining that every person consists of three parts: spirit, soul, and body. Through repentance and the renewal of the mind, believers are empowered to live according to the Spirit, walking in the authority granted by Christ. This book also underscores the vital role of speaking in tongues as a key to spiritual growth.

This book is essential for anyone who desires to deepen their relationship with God and experience the fullness of the Holy Spirit. The message it contains has the potential to revolutionize your prayer life, deepen your intimacy with God, and unlock new levels of spiritual power and understanding.

Pastor Sergie Atams
New Life Worship Center

CHAPTER 1

OPEN YOUR EYES

Many powerful events occurred inside you in the unseen *Realm of the Spirit* once you accepted Jesus Christ as your Lord and Saviour. For you to understand with your eyes of perception and see into this unseen realm, you must open the spiritual eyes of your heart through your imagination. The Bible has much to say about opening our eyes to see the unseen world and the invisible God. The Word of God also has much to say about who you are now as a new creation in Christ and what you have inherited. This book is an invaluable resource to help open the eyes of your heart to perceive the unseen world around you, see the invisible God, and discover who you are and what you have in the *Realm of the Spirit.*

When Jesus started His ministry, He spoke in parables to the crowds. Parables are simple short stories that illustrate spiritual lessons and truths through comparisons. All of the parables of Jesus intended to take what people knew and saw in the natural world and help them see into the unseen *Realm of the Spirit* and understand Divine truths. When considering the parables of Jesus, you must imagine what Jesus was teaching, transfer what you know, and see how it applies to the unseen world. Heavenly truths are hard for natural men and women to understand without the help of God and the use of their imagination.

Jesus only revealed the hidden spiritual meanings of parables to His closest disciples. When asked by one of His disciples why Jesus spoke in parables, He made a profound statement. Jesus said He spoke in parables because it wasn't given to the crowds to know God's mysteries since their hearts were "waxed gross," their ears were dull of hearing, and they closed their eyes.

> *Matthew 13:13-15 (KJV)*
> *13 **Therefore speak I to them in parables: because they seeing see not;** and hearing they hear not, neither do they understand. 14 And in them is fulfilled the prophecy of Esaias, which saith, By hearing ye shall hear, and shall not understand; **and seeing ye shall see, and shall not perceive:** 15 For this people's heart is waxed gross, and their ears are dull of hearing, **and their eyes they have closed; lest at any time they should see with their eyes** and hear with their ears, and should understand with their heart, and should be converted, and I should heal them.*

What was Jesus referring to when the disciples saw what the crowds were not seeing? We know the crowds saw the same miracles as the disciples did with their natural eyes, so it had to be more than the miracles. The disciples perceived with their spiritual eyes that Jesus was no ordinary man. They understood Jesus to be their long-awaited Messiah and Son of God. They also perceived, with the eyes of their understanding, the spiritual truths Jesus was teaching them. The crowds did not see Jesus for who He was and the spiritual truths He revealed about the mysteries of the Kingdom of God.

SOWER SOWS THE WORD

One of the most famous and important parables that Jesus ever preached about was the *"Sower Sows the Word."* This parable pictured a man throwing seed onto four different types of soil, representing four different types of hearts. This parable reveals the foundation to whoever wants to peer into the unseen *Realm of the Spirit*, see Christ in all His glory and understand Divine mysteries.

Let's explore the spiritual truths found in this parable and see the importance of what Jesus taught concerning the Kingdom of God in the parable of the *"Sower Sows the Word."* We will first read what He spoke to the crowds and then reveal what He later revealed to His disciples to gain insight into this thought-provoking parable.

> *Mark 4:2-9 (KJV)*
> *2 **And he taught them many things by parables**, and said unto them in his doctrine, 3 Hearken; Behold, there went out a sower to sow: 4 And it came to pass, as he sowed, some fell by the way side, and the fowls of the air came and devoured it up. 5 And some fell on stony ground, where it had not much earth; and immediately it sprang up, because it had no depth of earth: 6 But when the sun was up, it was scorched; and because it had no root, it withered away. 7 And some fell among thorns, and the thorns grew up, and choked it, and it yielded no fruit. 8 And other fell on good ground, and did yield fruit that sprang up and increased;*

and brought forth, some thirty, and some sixty, and some an
hundred. 9 And he said unto them, He that hath ears to hear,
let him hear.

This is the Divine hidden insight Jesus taught His disciples about this parable.

> **Mark 4:13-20 (KJV)**
> *13 And he said unto them, **Know ye not this parable? and***
> ***how then will ye know all parables?** 14 The sower soweth*
> *the word. 15 And these are they by the way side, where the*
> *word is sown; but when they have heard, Satan cometh*
> *immediately, and taketh away the word that was sown in*
> *their hearts. 16 And these are they likewise which are sown*
> *on stony ground; who, when they have heard the word,*
> *immediately receive it with gladness; 17 And have no root*
> *in themselves, and so endure but for a time: afterward, when*
> *affliction or persecution ariseth for the word's sake,*
> *immediately they are offended. 18 And these are they which*
> *are sown among thorns; such as hear the word, 19 And the*
> *cares of this world, and the deceitfulness of riches, and the*
> *lusts of other things entering in, choke the word, and it*
> *becometh unfruitful. 20 And these are they which are sown*
> *on good ground; such as hear the word, and receive it, and*
> *bring forth fruit, some thirtyfold, some sixty, and some an*
> *hundred.*

This simple yet powerful parable has many applications and spiritual truths. We want to explore how this parable applies when seeing into the *Realm of the Spirit*. This parable reveals that the seed, which represents the Word of God, is not the issue when it comes to people's ability to see with the eyes of their understanding the spiritual truths of the Kingdom of God that Jesus was teaching. Jesus taught this parable to reveal that the condition of the heart of the person receiving the Word of God determined their ability to perceive and see into the *Realm of the Spirit*. In this parable, Jesus placed the responsibility on the one hearing the Word of God to have a heart that could produce a harvest for the Kingdom of God.

Lack of understanding, commitment, and focus were the three conditions of the heart that caused the failure to produce a harvest. The first was a *"way side"* heart that didn't understand what was preached. The second heart was likened to stony ground, and when affliction or persecution arose for the Word of God's sake, they were offended because they had no root in themselves. The third heart was good ground, but weeds were allowed to grow up and choke the growing seed. The weeds represented the cares of this life, distractions, the deceitfulness of riches, and the lusts of other things.

Jesus revealed in this parable that He held the person receiving the Word of God responsible for opening the eyes of their heart to receive a hundredfold return on what was preached. This parable also reveals that our spiritual eyes can be opened by understanding, staying committed to, and focusing on the Word of God. The Word of God is the secret to seeing into the *Realm of the Spirit*. The more you read, look at, and understand the Word of God, the more you will see with your spiritual eyes into the *Realm of the Spirit*.

This parable should remain first and foremost in the thoughts of every believer throughout their entire life. The spiritual truths revealed in this parable never change and have profound implications for our success in serving God. Our lives as Christians should go from one spiritual eye-opening experience to another. There is no end to what God can reveal to you through the eyes of your understanding as you walk with Christ throughout your whole life. You are the only one responsible for seeking what God is saying in His Word and having a heart that produces the fruit of the Kingdom of God.

Many Christians seek to experience God in the natural realm and see spiritual things with their natural eyes. God, however, has chosen during this time for us not to see Him in the natural world. Miracles will manifest in the natural world along with answers to prayers, but you will not usually see an angel or God performing them with your naked eye. It's not to say God couldn't appear or Jesus show up in human form, He just doesn't for a reason.

When Jesus revealed Himself to Thomas after His resurrection, He said, *"Blessed are they that have not seen and yet have believed."* Jesus said this to Thomas because Thomas refused to believe unless he saw in His hands the print of nails, put his finger in the print of nails, and thrust his hand into His side.

> ### John 20:24-25 (KJV)
> *24 But Thomas, one of the twelve, called Didymus, was not with them when Jesus came. 25 The other disciples therefore said unto him, We have seen the Lord. But he said unto them,* **Except I shall see in his hands the print of the nails, and put my finger into the print of the nails, and thrust my hand into his side, I will not believe.**

Seeing with the inward eyes of your understanding and imagination has everything to do with your faith. Faith is believing God's Word without visible evidence in the natural world. It takes deep trust in your heart to believe the truth of what God says in His Word. Even if some people saw God and saw miracles with their natural eye, it doesn't mean they would believe and trust Him.

We can see this to be true by looking at the children of Israel who came out of Egypt. They saw God turn water into blood, supernaturally plague the Egyptians, part the Red Sea, water come out of a Rock, and many more miracles. They also saw God come down on Mount Sinai and audibly speak the Ten Commandments. None of these supernatural experiences produced faith in them, and they could not enter the Promised Land because of their unbelief. God said they were children who had no faith.

> ### Deuteronomy 32:20 (KJV)
> *20 And he said, I will hide my face from them, I will see what their end shall be: for they are a very froward generation,* **children in whom is no faith.**

You cannot please God in any other way except through faith.

> ### Hebrews 11:6 (KJV)
> *6* **But without faith it is impossible to please him***: for he that cometh to God must believe that he is, and that he is a rewarder of them that diligently seek him.*

Your faith enables you to see into the unseen *Realm of the Spirit* through the Word of God. Your faith is your inward eye that allows you to see with your imagination the invisible God and into the unseen *Realm of the Spirit*. We, as Christians, are called to walk by our faith, not by our natural eyes. When you walk by faith, you trust God and believe what He says is the truth. You can grow in your faith so that your spiritual eyes take over your natural eyes.

> ### *2 Corinthians 5:7 (KJV)*
> *7 (For we walk by faith, not by sight:)*

Everything in this natural world comes from the *Realm of the Spirit* and is controlled by the spiritual realm. When your eyes are opened and you are awakened to this truth, your life will never be the same. Jesus came as the Light of the World so you could see past the darkness and into His marvelous Light. You cannot see without light; without Christ, we cannot see into the *Realm of the Spirit.*

The Word of God teaches you who you are, and without the Word of God, you cannot know who you are in Christ. The Bible will not make sense to you if your spiritual eyes are not open where you can see into the *Realm of the Spirit.* The moment you believed in your heart that God raised Jesus from the dead, and you confessed Him as Lord, the Spirit of God created a new man in the exact image of the risen Christ in your spirit. From that point forward, the rest of your Christian life is a discovery of what took place inside you by renewing your mind so you can be transfigured into the image of Christ in your soul. As the Word of God renews your mind, you grow from a babe in Christ into a spiritually mature Christian. A fully mature Christian knows who they are in Christ and how to walk by faith through obedience to His Word.

In this book, we will reveal, by the Spirit of the Lord, how to see Christ in the Spirit, who you are in Christ, renew your mind, and teach you how to walk by faith and not by sight through your imagination. This book will be a discovery of the Word of God, and all that God created you to be when you accepted Christ as your Lord and Savior. The revelation of who you are in the Spirit will not only make you free but enable you to see the invisible God and operate in the unseen *Realm of the Spirit.* For this book to be effective, you must open your spiritual eyes and use your imagination to see all the powerful truths from the Word of God about who you are in Christ.

OPEN YOUR EYES AND SEE THE INVISIBLE GOD!

CHAPTER 2

IMAGE OF CHRIST

In this chapter, we will reveal Christ's appearance in the *Realm of the Spirit*. Christ in the Spirit looks much different than His physical human form. The Bible is very descriptive of the spiritual appearance of Christ in His Heavenly body. The eternal visual appearance of Christ in the *Realm of the Spirit* has never changed. But now, Christ has a resurrected body that can look similar to what He looked like before He went to the cross but can also change. In this chapter, you will discover the image of who you are in the *Realm of the Spirit* based on how Christ appears in His Heavenly body.

Before you can see and know who you are in the Spirit, you have to see and understand who Christ is in the *Realm of the Spirit.* The Bible reveals in the 1st Book of John that we don't know what we shall be like, but we know that when Christ appears, we shall be like Him, for we shall see Him as He is.

1 John 3:2 (KJV)

*2 Beloved, now are we the sons of God, **and it doth not yet appear what we shall be: but we know that, when he shall appear, we shall be like him; for we shall see him as he is.***

We know Christ first appeared in the unseen realm one way and appeared differently in His body while alive. We can see this truth when He took Peter, James, and John to the Mount of Transfiguration. When Jesus was on the Mount of Transfiguration, He was transfigured before them. His face shone like the sun, and His clothing was white as the light. Jesus was changing His appearance throughout the Gospels. We also know that Jesus hid and changed His appearance after His resurrection.

Matthew 17:1-2 (KJV)

1 And after six days Jesus taketh Peter, James, and John his brother, and bringeth them up into an high mountain apart,
*2 **And was transfigured before them: and his face did shine as the sun, and his raiment was white as the light.***

When Jesus was transfigured on the Mount of Transfiguration, He revealed who He was in the *Realm of the Spirit.* Jesus was shining like the sun the whole time He was on the Earth as a man, but in this experience, He allowed Peter, James, and John to see a glimpse of who He was in His unseen Heavenly form. The rest of humanity did not shine like the sun because Adam and Eve lost the glory of God that made them shine once they sinned in the Garden of Eden, and everyone born after them went dark.

When a sinner makes Jesus their Lord and repents of their sins, the Bible says Christ gives them light. When the repentant sinner receives this light, the Bible says it symbolizes them awakening from sleep and rising from the dead.

> ### Ephesians 5:13-14 (KJV)
> *13 But all things that are reproved are made manifest by the light: for whatsoever doth make manifest is light. 14* ***Wherefore he saith, Awake thou that sleepest, and arise from the dead, and Christ shall give thee light.***

It has always been God's desire for human beings to shine as He shines, but for this to occur, humankind must accept Christ, who is the Light of the world, and repent of their evil deeds. People who don't come to the light and repent of their evil deeds love darkness.

> ### John 3:19-21 (KJV)
> ***19 And this is the condemnation, that light is come into the world, and men loved darkness rather than light, because their deeds were evil. 20 For every one that doeth evil hateth the light, neither cometh to the light, lest his deeds should be reproved. 21 But he that doeth truth cometh to the light,*** *that his deeds may be made manifest, that they are wrought in God.*

When you confess Christ as your Lord and are born again, you are instantly made a son of God. Repenting of your sins reveals that you love the Light. The glory of God enters you by the Spirit of the Lord, and you begin to shine in the *Realm of the Spirit.* You will not fully see this until you see Jesus when He returns, or you pass on to the next life, but you shine like the sun with the glory of God now in your spirit.

Matthew 13:43 (KJV)

43 Then shall the righteous shine forth as the sun in the kingdom of their Father. *Who hath ears to hear, let him hear.*

Here are some New Testament verses that reveal that you are *"now"* shining and light in the Lord in the *Realm of the Spirit.*

Ephesians 5:8 (KJV)

8 For ye were sometimes darkness, but now are ye light in the Lord: walk as children of light:

Philippians 2:15 (KJV)

15 That ye may be blameless and harmless, the sons of God, without rebuke, in the midst of a crooked and perverse nation, **among whom ye shine as lights in the world;**

1 Peter 2:9 (KJV)

9 But ye are a chosen generation, a royal priesthood, an holy nation, a peculiar people; that ye should shew forth the praises of him **who hath called you out of darkness into his marvellous light;**

Matthew 5:14-16 (KJV)

14 **Ye are the light of the world.** *A city that is set on an hill cannot be hid. 15 Neither do men light a candle, and put it under a bushel, but on a candlestick; and it giveth light unto all that are in the house. 16* **Let your light so shine before men,** *that they may see your good works, and glorify your Father which is in heaven.*

The Old Testament Book of Isaiah prophesied that God's glory (light) would be seen upon us when *"gross darkness"* covered everyone else and over the Earth.

> ### *Isaiah 60:1-3 (KJV)*
> *1* ***Arise, shine; for thy light is come,*** *and the glory of the Lord is risen upon thee. 2* ***For, behold, the darkness shall cover the earth, and gross darkness the people:*** *but the Lord shall arise upon thee,* ***and his glory shall be seen upon thee. 3 And the Gentiles shall come to thy light****, and kings to the brightness of thy rising.*

In the Spirit, we look just like Jesus, but when we see Him, our bodies will be transformed to look like His resurrected body.

> ### *1 John 3:2 (KJV)*
> *2 Beloved, now are we the sons of God,* ***and it doth not yet appear what we shall be: but we know that, when he shall appear, we shall be like him; for we shall see him as he is.***

We are in a physical body, but our spirit is renewed instantly, and we are made a new creation the moment we make Jesus our Lord.

> ### *2 Corinthians 5:17 (KJV)*
> *17* ***Therefore if any man be in Christ, he is a new creature: old things are passed away; behold, all things are become new.***

The Bible says that we now have a natural body, but when we see Him when He appears, we will have a spiritual body. This is talking about our natural bodies and not who we are in the *Realm of the Spirit.* Our natural bodies will catch up and be quickened to resemble Jesus' resurrected body when we see Him.

1 Corinthians 15:39-49 (KJV)

*39 All flesh is not the same flesh: but there is one kind of flesh of men, another flesh of beasts, another of fishes, and another of birds. 40 There are also celestial bodies, and bodies terrestrial: but the glory of the celestial is one, and the glory of the terrestrial is another. 41 There is one glory of the sun, and another glory of the moon, and another glory of the stars: for one star differeth from another star in glory. 42 So also is the resurrection of the dead. It is sown in corruption; it is raised in incorruption: 43 It is sown in dishonour; it is raised in glory: it is sown in weakness; it is raised in power: 44 **It is sown a natural body; it is raised a spiritual body. There is a natural body, and there is a spiritual body.** 45 And so it is written, **The first man Adam was made a living soul; the last Adam was made a quickening spirit. 46 Howbeit that was not first which is spiritual, but that which is natural; and afterward that which is spiritual.** 47 The first man is of the earth, earthy; the second man is the Lord from heaven. 48 As is the earthy, such are they also that are earthy: and as is the heavenly, such are they also that are heavenly. 49 **And as we have borne the image of the earthy, we shall also bear the image of the heavenly.***

THE IMAGE OF CHRIST

Let's read in detail from the Word of God what Jesus looks like in the *Realm of the Spirit* so we can picture within ourselves what we look like. When reading these verses, you have to use your imagination to visualize Christ's appearance and then visualize yourself looking the same in your newly created spirit.

> ### *Ezekiel 1:26-27 (KJV)*
>
> *26 And above the firmament that was over their heads was the likeness of a throne, as the appearance of a sapphire stone: and upon the likeness of the throne was the likeness as the appearance of a man above upon it. 27 And I saw as the colour of amber, as the appearance of fire round about within it,* **from the appearance of his loins even upward, and from the appearance of his loins even downward, I saw as it were the appearance of fire, and it had brightness round about.**
>
> ### *Daniel 10:4-6 (KJV)*
>
> *4 And in the four and twentieth day of the first month, as I was by the side of the great river, which is Hiddekel; 5 Then I lifted up mine eyes, and looked,* **and behold a certain man clothed in linen, whose loins were girded with fine gold of Uphaz: 6 His body also was like the beryl, and his face as the appearance of lightning, and his eyes as lamps of fire, and his arms and his feet like in colour to polished brass,** *and the voice of his words like the voice of a multitude.*

Revelation 1:12-16 (KJV)

12 And I turned to see the voice that spake with me. And being turned, I saw seven golden candlesticks; 13 And in the midst of the seven candlesticks one like unto the Son of man, **clothed with a garment down to the foot, and girt about the paps with a golden girdle. 14 His head and his hairs were white like wool, as white as snow; and his eyes were as a flame of fire; 15 And his feet like unto fine brass, as if they burned in a furnace;** *and his voice as the sound of many waters. 16 And he had in his right hand seven stars: and out of his mouth went a sharp twoedged sword:* **and his countenance was as the sun shineth in his strength.**

Revelation 4:2-3 (KJV)

2 And immediately I was in the spirit: and, behold, a throne was set in heaven, and one sat on the throne. 3 **And he that sat was to look upon like a jasper and a sardine stone**: *and there was a rainbow round about the throne, in sight like unto an emerald.*

When we combine all of these verses, we see a complete picture of what Jesus looks like in the *Realm of the Spirit*. This is also how you look in the *Realm of the Spirit*.

HOW JESUS LOOKS IN THE SPIRIT

Our New Man is Created in His Same Image

1. Looks like a man

2. Looks like a jasper (glowing reddish) and sardine stone (glowing reddish)

3. Looks like the color of amber (like fire), with brightness around about and within from His loins upward and downward

4. Body like beryl (precious gemstone that looks emerald "sea-green" with various shades)

5. Clothed in linen down to His foot

6. Loins girded with fine golden girdle of Uphaz

7. Hair white like wool – white as snow

8. Face as the appearance of lightning

9. Eyes as lamps of fire (flames of fire)

10. Arms like polished brass (glowing)

11. Feet like polished fine brass as if they burned in a furnace (glowing)

12. Countenance as the sun shining in His strength (bright)

When you meditate on the image of Christ long enough with your imagination, it can profoundly affect how you see yourself. When you truly see who God has made you to be in the *Realm of the Spirit*, it can have a staggering effect on your self-esteem. You are seated in Heavenly places as a son of God in Christ Jesus with a spiritual body that looks just like Him. This is who you are *"now"* in the *Realm of the Spirit!* This is a present reality for every believer! You are not a helpless victim with no power. You are made in the image of Christ, a very powerful spiritual being. Jesus paid a heavy price so we could be created new in His image.

In conclusion, we can see there is more to being a Christian than what meets the natural eye. You can never be the same when you read the Word of God and discover who you are. The beauty of this is we don't have to wait to go to Heaven for this to be a reality. This is who God made you to be in the Spirit realm when you make Christ your Lord and Saviour. You are a powerful son of God made in the image of Christ, and you shine like the sun *NOW* in the *Realm of the Spirit!*

THE ONLY WAY TO BE TRANSFORMED IN THE IMAGE OF CHRIST IS TO LOOK AT HIM IN THE REALM OF THE SPIRIT!

CHAPTER 3

THE WORDS OF JESUS

In the previous chapter, we brought to light what Jesus looks like in the Spirit, and what we look like in the *Realm of the Spirit*. What Jesus looks like is His image, but the word image reveals more than what someone looks like on the outside, but who they also are on the inside. Jesus appears one way in the *Realm of the Spirit* and a different way in His natural body, but the image of **WHO HE IS** is unchanging. An image of who someone is can be made known by what they live, speak, and teach. In this chapter, we will reveal the glory of God in the image of who Christ is through His *Core Teachings*, *Parables*, *Commands*, and *Words*.

Jesus revealed who He was, what He stood for, His belief systems, and what He believed about right and wrong in His ministry whenever He taught and preached the Word of God. When Jesus proclaimed the *TRUTH*, He revealed the glorious image and essence of Who He, the Father, and the Holy Spirit are. The Image of God and His Divine Nature is hidden and encoded in Christ's Teachings, Parables, Commands, and Words. The glorious character in the way He thinks and acts makes God shine like the sun. This is also what makes Christians shine. God loves righteousness and hates evil. God is majestic and shines like the brightness of the sun because all His ways are *Wise, Righteous, Just, Perfect*, and *Loving*.

When the Bible refers to Jesus being the express image of the Godhead, it refers to His glorious Divine nature.

> ### Hebrews 1:3 (KJV)
> **3 Who being the brightness of his glory, and the express image of his person,** *and upholding all things by the word of his power, when he had by himself purged our sins, sat down on the right hand of the Majesty on high:*

> ### Colossians 1:14-15 (KJV)
> *14 In whom we have redemption through his blood, even the forgiveness of sins: 15* **Who is the image of the invisible God,** *the firstborn of every creature:*

It is impossible to explain the whole Divine nature of God in one sentence. Jesus had to preach and teach for many years to paint the complete picture of who He, the Father, and the Holy Spirit are. As you read the Gospels (Matthew, Mark, Luke, and John), you can see the glorious Divine nature of God as revealed in the Words of Christ. Christ revealed who He was as He preached the *Good News* and taught the Word of God. He also manifested His *glorious* nature of grace and truth by living out His life before His disciples. Jesus is the complete living embodiment of God, who He is, and what He stands for by the Spirit of the Lord.

John 1:1 (KJV)

*1 **In the beginning was the Word, and the Word was with God, and the Word was God.***

John 1:14 (KJV)

*14 And the Word was made flesh, and dwelt among us, **(and we beheld his glory, the glory as of the only begotten of the Father,)** full of grace and truth.*

Jesus placed great importance on His Words and our obedience to them. His very Words are the containers of the glorious image of God. He said Heaven and Earth would pass away, but His Words would not pass away (Matthew 24:35). He also said He would not judge us on Judgment Day, but His Words would judge us. It is extremely imperative as Christians to hear, study, live, and become the Words of Christ.

John 12:47-49 (KJV)

*47 **And if any man hear my words, and believe not, I judge him not: for I came not to judge the world, but to save the world.** 48 **He that rejecteth me, and receiveth not my words, hath one that judgeth him: the word that I have spoken, the same shall judge him in the last day.** 49 For I have not spoken of myself; but the Father which sent me, he gave me a commandment, what I should say, and what I should speak.*

We have gathered the core teachings of Christ into a simplified list so you can see an overview of the image of God through His Words. It is spiritually vital to go over each verse and read it for yourself to paint an inner image of who God is so you can pattern your life after His image that is revealed by His Words. The Bible teaches that as we look at the glorious image of God, we are changed into His exact image from glory to glory. We can see the glory of God by reading, looking at, and meditating on the Words of Christ. This is also called mind renewal, and we will get into more detail about how to renew your mind in Chapter Seven.

> *2 Corinthians 3:18 (KJV)*
> *18 **But we all, with open face beholding as in a glass the glory of the Lord, are changed into the same image from glory to glory, even as by the Spirit of the Lord.***

Meditate with your imagination as you read the Core Teachings of Christ below. Look at the teaching itself, and afterward, look at the verse listed and meditate on them. Examine yourself to see if you are living the truth of the *Glorious Image* of what Jesus taught. Remember, the Core Teachings of Jesus are going to be the standard God uses to Judge all of humanity on Judgment Day, so pay close attention to each one and conform your words and actions to imitate the glory of God. God expects you to live the Words of Christ. Everyone who hears and does the Words of Christ is likened to a man who built his house upon a rock and survived a storm.

> *Matthew 7:24-27 (KJV)*
> *24 Therefore whosoever heareth these sayings of mine, and doeth them, I will liken him unto a wise man, which built his house upon a rock: 25 And the rain descended, and the floods came, and the winds blew, and beat upon that house; and it fell not: for it was founded upon a rock. 26 **And every one that heareth these sayings of mine, and doeth them***

not, shall be likened unto a foolish man, which built his house upon the sand: 27 And the rain descended, and the floods came, and the winds blew, and beat upon that house; and it fell: and great was the fall of it.

CORE TEACHINGS OF CHRIST

1. Repent (Mark 1:15)

2. Believe the Gospel (Mark 1:15)

3. If you believe on Him, you are given the power to be a son of God (John 1:12)

4. Whoever believes on Him and is baptized shall be saved (Mark 16:16)

5. Whoever believes on Him will not perish but receive Eternal Life (John 3:16)

6. If you do not believe, you are damned (Mark 16:16)

7. Observe all things He Commanded us to do (Matthew 28:20)

8. Take up your cross daily, deny yourself, and follow Him (Luke 9:23)

9. If you do not take up your cross daily, you are not worthy of Him (Matthew 10:38)

10. Visit those in prison (Matthew 25:36)

11. Feed the hungry (Matthew 25:35)

12. Give the thirsty something to drink (Matthew 25:35)

13. Take in strangers (Matthew 25:35)

14. Visit the sick (Matthew 25:36)

15. Clothe the naked (Matthew 25:36)

16. Hold banquets for the poor, maimed, lame, and blind (Luke 14:12-14)

17. Lend, expecting nothing in return (Luke 6:34-35)

18. Recover the sick by laying hands on them (Mark 16:18)

19. Cast out devils in the Name of Jesus Christ (Mark 16:17)

20. Be wise and have oil in your lamps, expecting His return (Matthew 25:1-12)

21. Don't give your oil away to foolish virgins while waiting for the return of Christ (Matthew 25:8-10)

22. If you deny Him, He will deny you before the Father (Matthew 10:33)

23. Love God above your family members (Matthew 10:36-37)

24. He that findeth his life shall lose it: and he that loseth his life for Jesus shall find it (Matthew 10:39)

25. Blessed are the poor in spirit: for theirs is the kingdom of Heaven (Matthew 5:3)

26. Blessed are they that mourn, for they shall be comforted (Matthew 5:4)

27. Blessed are the meek: for they shall inherit the Earth (Matthew 5:5)

28. Blessed are they which do hunger and thirst after righteousness: for they shall be filled (Matthew 5:6)

29. Blessed are the merciful: for they shall obtain mercy (Matthew 5:7)

30. Blessed are the pure in heart: for they shall see God (Matthew 5:8)

31. Blessed are the peacemakers: for they shall be called the children of God (Matthew 5:9)

32. Blessed are they which are persecuted for righteousness' sake: for theirs is the Kingdom of Heaven (Matthew 5:10)

33. Rejoice and be exceedingly glad when you are persecuted (Matthew 5:12)

34. Let your light shine before men that others will see your good works and glorify your Father in Heaven (Matthew 5:16)

35. Whoever humbles themselves as a little child is the greatest in the Kingdom of Heaven (Matthew 18:4)

36. It is the will of the Father that none should perish (Matthew 18:14)

37. Woe unto the world because of offenses (Matthew 18:7)

38. Forgive others their trespasses from the heart
    (Matthew 18:23-35)

39. Unforgiveness will hinder your prayers of faith
    (Mark 11:25-26)

40. Forgive seventy-seven times (unlimited forgiveness)
    (Matthew 18:21-22)

41. If you do not forgive, you will not be forgiven (Matthew 6:15)

42. Love one another (John 15:17)

43. Love your enemies (Matthew 5:44)

44. Bless them that curse you (Matthew 5:44)

45. Do good to them that hate you (Matthew 5:44)

46. Pray for them which despitefully use you, and persecute you
    (Matthew 5:44)

47. Whosoever shall smite thee on thy right cheek, turn to him the
    other also (Matthew 5:39)

48. If any man will sue thee at the law, and take away your coat, let
    him have your cloak also (Matthew 5:40)

49. Whosoever shall compel you to go a mile, go with him two
    (Matthew 5:41)

50. Be a good Samaritan (have compassion and help others in need) (Luke 10:30-37)

51. Give to whoever asks of you (Matthew 5:42)

52. Give to whoever would borrow from you (Matthew 5:42)

53. Give, and it will be given unto you with the same measure that you mete (Luke 6:38)

54. Be perfect even as your Father in Heaven is perfect (Matthew 5:48)

55. Live prepared for the return of Christ (Luke 12:35-48)

56. Keep your lamps burning (Luke 12:35)

57. Keep your loins girded (Luke 12:35)

58. Jesus is going to return unexpectedly and reward those who are waiting for Him (Luke 12:46)

59. Jesus is going to return unexpectedly and judge those not ready (Luke 12:46-48)

60. Whatever you did to the least of the brethren you did to Christ (Matthew 25:31-46)

61. Don't lay-up treasures on Earth (Matthew 6:19)

62. Lay-up treasures in Heaven (Matthew 6:20)

63. Have faith in God (Mark 11:22)

64. You only need faith the size of a mustard seed to move a mountain (Matthew 17:20)

65. If you have faith the size of a mustard seed, nothing will be impossible to you (Matthew 17:20)

66. You can speak to mountains and make them move with your faith-filled words (Mark 11:23)

67. Believe you have received when you pray (Mark 11:24)

68. Out of the abundance of the heart, the mouth speaks (Matthew 12:34)

69. You will be judged for every idle word you speak on Judgment Day (Matthew 12:36)

70. You will be justified or condemned by your words (Matthew 12:37)

71. Be persistent in prayer (Luke 18:1-8)

72. We should always pray (Luke 18:1)

73. Never faint when praying (Luke 18:1)

74. Ask, and you will receive (Matthew 7:7-8)

75. Seek, and you will find (Matthew 7:7-8)

76. Knock, and it will be opened to you (Matthew 7:7-8)

77. The Father will give the Holy Spirit to them that ask of Him (Luke 11:11-13)

78. Those who believe in Him would do greater works than He did (John 14:12)

79. Beware of covetousness (greed) (Luke 12:15)

80. If you are not with Christ, you are against Him (Matthew 12:30)

81. You cannot serve two masters (Matthew 6:24)

82. You cannot serve God and money (Matthew 6:24)

83. The Kingdom of God is at hand (Matthew 3:2)

84. You must be born again to see the Kingdom of God (John 3:3)

85. You must be born of water and the Spirit to enter the Kingdom of God (John 3:5)

86. The Kingdom of God is within you (Luke 17:20-21)

87. Seek first the Kingdom of God and His righteousness (Matthew 6:33)

88. Press into the Kingdom of God (Luke 16:16)

89. The Kingdom of Heaven suffers violence and is taken by force (Matthew 11:12)

90. It is the Father's good pleasure to give you the Kingdom (Luke 12:32)

91. He that is least in the Kingdom of Heaven is greater than John the Baptist (Matthew 11:11)

92. To reap a hundredfold return in the Kingdom of God, you must first understand His Words (Matthew 13:19)

93. To reap a hundredfold return in the Kingdom of God, you must survive tribulation and persecution for His Words (Matthew 13:21)

94. To reap a hundredfold return in the Kingdom of God, you must not be distracted by the cares of this world, the deceitfulness of riches, and the lust of other things (Mark 4:18-19)

95. If you continue in His Words, you are His disciple (John 8:31)

96. His disciples will know the truth and be made free (John 8:32)

97. The Words of Jesus will never pass away (Matthew 24:35)

98. The Words Jesus spoke were Spirit and Life (John 6:63)

99. You cannot do anything without Christ (John 15:5)

100. Jesus came to give us Abundant Life (John 10:10)

101. If we abide in Christ and His Words abide in us, we shall ask whatever we will, and it will be done (John 15:7)

102. God gave us the glory of God (John 17:22)

103. We are one with Christ and the Father (John 17:22)

104. The Father loves us as much as He loves Jesus (John 17:23)

105. You are wise if you hear and do the words of Christ (Matthew 7:24)

106. Those who build their lives on the Words of Christ will survive storms (Matthew 7:24-25)

107. Those who don't hear and do the Words of Christ are foolish (Matthew 7:26)

108. Those who don't hear and do the Words of Christ will be destroyed by a storm (Matthew 7:26-27)

109. Only those who do the will of the Father in Heaven will enter into the Kingdom of Heaven (Matthew 7:21)

110. Don't seek after signs (Matthew 12:39)

111. That which is highly esteemed among men is an abomination in the sight of God (Luke 16:15)

112. Take heed that no one deceives you (Matthew 24:4)

113. Beware of false prophets (Matthew 7:15)

114. You will know a false prophet by his fruits (Matthew 7:15-16)

115. Don't be deceived by a false Christ (Matthew 24:5)

116. Only the Father knows when Christ will return (Matthew 24:36)

117. His sheep know His voice and will not follow the voice of strangers (John 10:1-5)

118. Receive the Holy Spirit (John 20:22)

119. The Holy Spirit will come and teach us all things that Jesus taught (John 14:26)

120. The Holy Spirit is our Comforter and will abide with us forever (John 14:16)

121. You have to be baptized in the Holy Spirit to receive power for witnessing (Acts 1:8)

122. You will never be forgiven if you blaspheme the Holy Spirit (Matthew 12:31-32)

123. Take no thought about what you will drink (Matthew 6:31)

124. Take no thought about what you will eat (Matthew 6:31)

125. Take no thought about what you will wear (Matthew 6:31)

126. Take no thought about tomorrow (Matthew 6:34)

127. Those that will believe will cast out devils (Mark 16:17)

128. Those who believe will speak with new tongues (Mark 16:17)

129. Those who believe will take up serpents (Mark 16:18)

130. Those who believe will not be harmed by drinking any deadly thing (Mark 16:18)

131. Lay hands on the sick, and they will recover (Mark 16:18)

132. Your righteousness must exceed the righteousness of the Scribes & Pharisees (Matthew 5:20)

133. Whoever teaches the Commandments of God will be called great in the Kingdom of Heaven (Matthew 5:17-19)

134. Lusting after women with your eyes is adultery (Matthew 5:27-30)

135. Don't be angry at your brother without a cause and call him a fool (Matthew 5:21-22)

136. Agree with your adversary quickly (Matthew 5:25-26)

137. Judge not lest you be judged (Matthew 7:1-5)

138. Be not ye called Rabbi: for one is your Master, even Christ; and all ye are brethren (Matthew 23:8)

139. Call no man your father upon the earth: for one is your Father, which is in Heaven (Matthew 23:9)

140. Be not called masters: for one is your Master, even Christ (Matthew 23:10)

141. The servant of all is the greatest of all (Matthew 23:11)

142. Whoever exalts himself will be abased (Matthew 23:12)

143. Whoever humbles themselves will be exalted (Matthew 23:12)

144. Give in secret (Matthew 6:1-4)

145. Pray in secret (Matthew 6:5-6)

146. Fast in secret (Matthew 6:16-18)

147. Don't use vain repetitions when you pray (Matthew 6:7-8)

148. Don't swear (Matthew 5:33-37)

149. Don't divorce except for fornication (Matthew 5:31-32)

150. Do unto others as you would want done unto yourself (Matthew 7:12)

151. Love God with all of your heart, soul, mind and strength (Mark 12:28-30)

152. Love your neighbor as yourself (Mark 12:31)

153. Preach the Gospel (Good News) to every creature (Mark 16:15)

This list is a resource you can use throughout your life to examine yourself. We cannot express enough the importance of becoming the image of Christ. The best way to mature into the image of Christ is by hearing, reading, studying, and obeying all things He Commanded us in His Word.

> **Matthew 28:19-20 (KJV)**
> *19 Go ye therefore, and teach all nations, baptizing them in the name of the Father, and of the Son, and of the Holy*

*Ghost: 20 **Teaching them to observe all things whatsoever
I have commanded you:** and, lo, I am with you always, even
unto the end of the world. Amen.*

Jesus revealed to Martha that what you receive and become by hearing
and obeying the Words of Christ can never be taken from you, when her
sister Mary chose to sit at the feet of Jesus and listen to His teachings
above serving at that moment with Martha.

> *Luke 10:38-42 (KJV)*
>
> *38 Now it came to pass, as they went, that he entered into a
> certain village: and a certain woman named Martha
> received him into her house. 39 **And she had a sister called
> Mary, which also sat at Jesus' feet, and heard his word.** 40
> But Martha was cumbered about much serving, and came
> to him, and said, Lord, dost thou not care that my sister hath
> left me to serve alone? bid her therefore that she help me.
> 41 And Jesus answered and said unto her, Martha, Martha,
> thou art careful and troubled about many things: 42 **But one
> thing is needful: and Mary hath chosen that good part,
> which shall not be taken away from her.***

THE DIVINE NATURE

Jesus came to reveal and impart God's Divine Nature to His followers.
We become partakers of God's Divine Nature as we grow in God's Word
and partake of His exceeding great and precious promises. As you hear,
understand, and obey Christ's teachings and commands, you are changed
into the very image of the Words that Christ spoke. The secret to
becoming like God is found in the promises of His Word.

2 Peter 1:3-4 (KJV)

3 According as his divine power hath given unto us all things that pertain unto life and godliness, through the knowledge of him that hath called us to glory and virtue:

4 Whereby are given unto us exceeding great and precious promises: that by these ye might be partakers of the divine nature, having escaped the corruption that is in the world through lust.

In summary, you can see how Jesus revealed God's glorious nature and image in what He taught. All true Christians hear and observe to do all things that Jesus taught. The mystery of who God is can be found in the Words of Christ, and Jesus was our living example of how to be like God. We must hear, read, and obey His Words to become like God. Your greatest accomplishment will be to build your life on all the Words of Christ! We pray this chapter has helped you see God's image in the Words of Christ and how you can come into the same image of Christ as you obey all of His Words.

THE EXPRESS IMAGE OF THE FATHER IS ENCODED IN THE WORDS OF CHRIST!

CHAPTER 4

SPIRIT, SOUL & BODY

This is a pivotal chapter of this book, and if you can grasp the truths found here with the eyes of your spiritual understanding, you will be able to comprehend secrets to the New Testament and who you are in Christ. To fully comprehend the new birth in Christ, you must know you are comprised of three parts: spirit, soul, and body. Once you know these three parts of your being, you can begin to see who you truly are in the *Realm of the Spirit* and how the new birth impacts your soul and body.

When you made Jesus your Lord and Saviour, your spirit was born again, but your soul and body were not. Your soul needs to be renewed, and your body needs to be quickened. When believers do not know and misunderstand the three parts of their being, they can misinterpret many Bible verses concerning the new birth. When reading the Bible, you need to know which part of your being is being talked about to understand the depth of what is being taught.

You must understand that you are a spirit, have a soul, and live in a body. Your spirit connects you to the unseen *Realm of the Spirit,* your body connects you to the natural world you live in, and your soul is the conduit between your spirit and body. An important verse in the Bible that helps us to understand that we are a three-part being is found in 1 Thessalonians 5:23.

> *1 Thessalonians 5:23 (KJV)*
> *23 And the very God of peace sanctify you wholly; and I pray God your whole spirit and soul and body be preserved blameless unto the coming of our Lord Jesus Christ.*

1 John 3:9 is an excellent example of a verse that is sometimes misunderstood and misinterpreted because it talks about your spirit when some think it is referencing your soul. This verse says that whoever is born of God cannot sin. When you understand that there are three parts to your being, you know that this is talking about your spirit that was newly created in the image of Christ. Your newly created born-again spirit cannot sin. Your soul and body can potentially sin.

> *1 John 3:9 (KJV)*
> *9 Whosoever is born of God doth not commit sin; for his seed remaineth in him: and he cannot sin, because he is born of God.*

There is another verse in this same book that seems to contradict this verse. 1 John 1:8-10 says, *"If we say we have no sin or have not sinned, we make him a liar."* This refers to your body and soul, which can sin. Now that you know the distinction between your soul, body, and spirit, this verse can be understood and interpreted correctly.

> *1 John 1:8-10 (KJV)*
>
> *8 **If we say that we have no sin, we deceive ourselves,** and the truth is not in us. 9 If we confess our sins, he is faithful and just to forgive us our sins, and to cleanse us from all unrighteousness. 10 **If we say that we have not sinned, we make him a liar,** and his word is not in us.*

Once you recognize the difference between your spirit, soul, and body, the Bible becomes more understandable, and many verses you didn't grasp before will make sense. Now, you can see your spirit as separate from your soul and body, but it is still the *New You*. It is also crucial to realize that what you look at you become, so as you look into the *Realm of the Spirit* and see you are sinless, you will become less prone to sin by knowing Jesus made your newly created spirit sinless. Those who continue to look to their body and soul will never fully experience the righteousness of God in Christ Jesus. You must look into the *Realm of the Spirit* and see that God made the *New Man* sinless and perfect to experience the righteousness of God.

> *1 Corinthians 1:30 (KJV)*
>
> *30 **But of him are ye in Christ Jesus, who of God is made unto us** wisdom, **and righteousness**, and sanctification, and redemption:*

> *Philippians 3:9 (KJV)*
>
> *9 **And be found in him, not having mine own righteousness,** which is of the law, but that which is through the faith of Christ, **the righteousness which is of God by faith:***

The Bible also says we have an unction (anointing), and we know all things. This would seem untrue to someone who lives only out of their soul. Your soul does not know everything; however, your spirit man, connected to the Holy Spirit, knows everything. God knows all things, and because your spirit was created to be one with God, you know all things.

>*1 John 2:20 (KJV)*
>*20 But ye have an unction from the Holy One, and ye know all things.*

Understanding the difference between your soul, body, and spirit helps you comprehend many Bible verses concerning your spirit. You can tap into the all-knowing knowledge of God at any time by faith, but you must perceive this will only take place through the anointing. A born-again believer can never say they are in the dark. Their soul may be in the dark, but their spirit is not in the dark because of the anointing. You are no longer just a soul and body with a dead spirit. Your spirit was quickened and made alive through the anointing that teaches you all things.

>*1 John 2:27 (KJV)*
>*27 But the anointing which ye have received of him abideth in you, and ye need not that any man teach you: but as the same anointing teacheth you of all things, and is truth, and is no lie, and even as it hath taught you, ye shall abide in him.*

NEW BIRTH

When Jesus told Nicodemus to see the Kingdom of God, you must be born again, He was referring to the new birth of the spirit man. Nicodemus was confused because he didn't perceive that Jesus was teaching the concept of the difference between spirit, soul, and body. Nicodemus thought Jesus was talking about his body being reborn and didn't understand that Jesus was talking about a rebirth in the *Realm of the Spirit.*

> ### *John 3:1-10 (KJV)*
>
> *1 There was a man of the Pharisees, named Nicodemus, a ruler of the Jews: 2 The same came to Jesus by night, and said unto him, Rabbi, we know that thou art a teacher come from God: for no man can do these miracles that thou doest, except God be with him. 3 **Jesus answered and said unto him, Verily, verily, I say unto thee, Except a man be born again, he cannot see the kingdom of God. 4 Nicodemus saith unto him, How can a man be born when he is old? can he enter the second time into his mother's womb, and be born? 5 Jesus answered, Verily, verily, I say unto thee, Except a man be born of water and of the Spirit, he cannot enter into the kingdom of God. 6 That which is born of the flesh is flesh; and that which is born of the Spirit is spirit. 7 Marvel not that I said unto thee, Ye must be born again.** 8 The wind bloweth where it listeth, and thou hearest the sound thereof, but canst not tell whence it cometh, and whither it goeth: so is every one that is born of the Spirit. 9 Nicodemus answered and said unto him, How can these*

*things be? 10 **Jesus answered and said unto him, Art thou
a master of Israel, and knowest not these things?***

Once Adam ate from the Tree of the Knowledge of Good and Evil, his
spirit man died. Then, Adam's body later died, and his soul experienced
death when it went to hell. Also, everyone born after Adam was born
with a dead spirit, except for Christ because he was born of a virgin.
Jesus had to reverse the curse of death by becoming a curse for us by
dying on a tree and going to hell. When Jesus healed people, they were
experiencing the life of God in their bodies, but the body does eventually
die. Once Jesus returns, we will enter into the manifested Kingdom of
God on the Earth in resurrected bodies, and there will be no more death
in our spirits, souls, or bodies. The last enemy to be destroyed will be
death.

> *1 Corinthians 15:20-28 (KJV)*
> *20 But now is Christ risen from the dead, and become the
> firstfruits of them that slept. 21 For since by man came
> death, by man came also the resurrection of the dead. 22
> **For as in Adam all die, even so in Christ shall all be made
> alive.** 23 But every man in his own order: Christ the
> firstfruits; afterward they that are Christ's at his coming. 24
> Then cometh the end, when he shall have delivered up the
> kingdom to God, even the Father; when he shall have put
> down all rule and all authority and power. 25 For he must
> reign, till he hath put all enemies under his feet. 26 **The last
> enemy that shall be destroyed is death.** 27 For he hath put
> all things under his feet. But when he saith all things are put
> under him, it is manifest that he is excepted, which did put*

all things under him. 28 And when all things shall be
subdued unto him, then shall the Son also himself be subject
unto him that put all things under him, that God may be all
in all.

Death was a blessing in disguise because, through death, we have the
opportunity to be reborn. Humanity has been given the opportunity to
start afresh in Christ through His death. When you repent of your sins,
you are reborn and given a second chance. Angels are not given the
opportunity of being born again when they sin because they are eternal
beings and don't die as humans do.

SEALED BY THE HOLY SPIRIT

As a born-again believer, your spirit is newly created and sealed by the
Holy Spirit. This means nothing in your spirit can get out, and nothing
can get in. The Holy Spirit protects your newly created spirit, that lives
within your soul and body.

> *2 Corinthians 1:22 (KJV)*
> *22 **Who hath also sealed us, and given the earnest of the***
> ***Spirit in our hearts.***

The sealing of the Holy Spirit is your guarantee and down payment of
redemption before you enter Heaven.

> *Ephesians 1:13-14 (KJV)*
> *13 In whom ye also trusted, after that ye heard the word of*
> *truth, the gospel of your salvation: in whom also after that*
> *ye believed, **ye were sealed with that holy Spirit of promise,***
> *14 Which is the earnest of our inheritance until the*

redemption of the purchased possession, unto the praise of his glory.

Everything within your spirit is hidden, and it takes revelation from the Word of God by the Holy Spirit for you to see who you are in Christ and what you have. Without Divine revelation, we will never fully know who we are and what we have been given in the *Realm of the Spirit.*

> *1 Corinthians 2:9-10 (KJV)*
> *9 But as it is written, Eye hath not seen, nor ear heard, neither have entered into the heart of man, the things which God hath prepared for them that love him. 10 But God hath revealed them unto us by his Spirit: for the Spirit searcheth all things, yea, the deep things of God.*

When you don't know who you are and what you have, you can be destroyed for your lack of knowledge (Hosea 4:6). Destroyed means go without healing and deliverance in areas of your soul and body when you don't need to go without. What good is it to have something but not know you have it? Also, what good is it to have something but not know how to access or use what you have? It's like not having it at all! We must learn all we can about the *New Man* and what we have in the *Realm of the Spirit* so that we can inherit all of the promises of God.

God wants His people to know what they have and how to access it. This, however, can only be done by renewing your mind to the Word of God, which takes work and spiritual effort on your part. We can help you see who you are and what you have as ministers by the Spirit of the Lord, but it is your responsibility to renew your mind and protect your heart. In the chapter, *Mind Renewal*, we will teach you secrets on how to renew your mind to the *Realm of the Spirit*. In the chapter, *Imagination*, we will teach you how to use your imagination effectively to see who you are and what God has given freely. In the chapter called *Acknowledgements*, we will teach you how to acknowledge what you already have so your faith can effectively inherit all that God has given and made you to be.

Your soul prospers when you renew your mind to who you are in the spirit. Through a correct understanding of the new you, your soul matures into the image of Christ. As you grow in Christ and your soul aligns with the truth of who God made you to be in Christ, you enter into new dimensions of the Spirit, which causes the blessings of God to enter your soul, manifest in your body, and change the world around you.

> *3 John 1:2 (KJV)*
> *2 Beloved, I wish above all things that thou mayest prosper and be in health, even as thy soul prospereth.*

THE REST OF GOD

God has done everything He can and will do for you, and it is up to you to enter His *REST*. Entering the *REST of God* means you cease from your own works and believe everything was accomplished in Christ when He died, was buried, and rose again. This means that you acknowledge God has done everything He will do and wrote them down in His Word for us to study and know what we have. However, we are all responsible for entering into His *REST* by believing He has already done whatever we need. This is expressed in the Word of God as working out your own salvation with fear and trembling.

Philippians 2:12 (KJV)

*12 Wherefore, my beloved, as ye have always obeyed, not as in my presence only, but now much more in my absence, **work out your own salvation with fear and trembling.***

Another way the Bible teaches this truth is when it talks about us laboring to enter into the *Rest of God*. Our labor is not like you think. We are not laboring to get God to do anything He hasn't already done. Our labor has more to do with our souls inheriting the promises of God. We must receive the Word of God and live it to inherit all that God has done. The Word of God is given to show us who we are and what we have. We take these truths and live out what God put in us, which God considers our labor.

Hebrews 4:11-12 (KJV)

*11 **Let us labour therefore to enter into that rest,** lest any man fall after the same example of unbelief. 12 For the word of God is quick, and powerful, and sharper than any twoedged sword, piercing even to the dividing asunder of soul and spirit, and of the joints and marrow, and is a discerner of the thoughts and intents of the heart.*

You entering the *REST* of God has everything to do with you seeing and receiving by faith what He has already done. No work of the flesh can be done to inherit the promises of God because they have already been freely given; you must receive them by faith.

Hebrews 4:1-7 (KJV)

*1 **Let us therefore fear, lest, a promise being left us of entering into his rest, any of you should seem to come*** *short of it. 2 **For unto us was the gospel preached, as well as unto them: but the word preached did not profit them, not being mixed with faith in them that heard it. 3 For we which have believed do enter into rest,** as he said, As I have sworn in my wrath, if they shall enter into my rest: although the works were finished from the foundation of the world. 4 For he spake in a certain place of the seventh day on this wise, And God did rest the seventh day from all his works. 5 And in this place again, **If they shall enter into my rest. 6 Seeing therefore it remaineth that some must enter therein, and they to whom it was first preached entered not in because of unbelief:** 7 Again, he limiteth a certain day, saying in David, To day, after so long a time; as it is said, To day if ye will hear his voice, harden not your hearts.*

When Jesus said, **"IT IS FINISHED"** on the cross, everything concerning our redemption was completed. Everything we will ever receive from God has already been given to us, which was placed in our spirit when we made Jesus our Lord. We must learn how to receive with our faith what God has freely given us in the *Realm of the Spirit*. Faith brings spiritual blessings from the unseen realm into our souls and bodies.

Ephesians 1:17-20 (KJV)

*17 That the God of our Lord Jesus Christ, the Father of glory, may give unto you the spirit of wisdom and revelation in the knowledge of him: 18 **The eyes of your understanding being enlightened; that ye may know what is the hope of his calling, and what the riches of the glory*** *of his inheritance in the saints, 19 And what is the exceeding greatness of his power to us-ward who believe, according to the working of his mighty power, 20 Which he wrought in Christ, when he raised him from the dead, and set him at his own right hand in the heavenly places,*

We compiled a list of what the *New Man* has in your spirit. This list can be referred to repeatedly until your mind is renewed to who you are and what you have. As your eyes are opened, you are changed in your soul, mind, and body to the new realities you have in Christ. God has destined you to take His truths and allow them to change you from the inside out. You don't need God to do anything else for you. You need to learn to receive and implement what He has already done with the help of the Holy Spirit, and this is what the Bible calls *"Entering His Rest."*

NEW MAN

1. Looks Like the Risen Lord's Glorified Body - 1 John 3:1-3; Ezekiel 1:26-27; Daniel 10:4-6; Revelation 1:12-16

2. Son of God - John 1:12; 1 John 3:1-3

3. New Creation – 2 Corinthians 5:17

4. Risen with Christ – Romans 8:11; Colossians 3:1-4

5. Made in the Image of Christ – Romans 8:29

6. Shines like the Sun – Matthew 13:43

7. Temple of the Holy Spirit – 1 Corinthians 3:16-17; 1 Corinthians 6:19-20; 2 Corinthians 6:14-18

8. Filled With the Holy Spirit – Ephesians 5:18

9. Has the Glory of God – John 17:22-24; Isaiah 60:1-3; Ephesians 1:17-18; Exodus 33:18-23; Exodus 34:5-7

10. One With God – John 17:20-23

11. Joined as One Spirit with the Lord – 1 Corinthians 6:17

12. Knows God – John 17:3

13. Has Everlasting Life – John 3:16

14. Has the Resurrection Power of God – Acts 1:8; Acts 4:33; Romans 8:11; Philippians 3:10

15. Blessed with all Spiritual Blessings in Heavenly Places in Christ – Ephesians 1:3

16. Can Do All Things Through Christ – Philippians 4:13

17. Can Speak to Mountains and Make them Move – Matthew 17:20; Matthew 21:21-22; Mark 11:22-24

18. Can Do the Impossible – Matthew 17:20

19. Can Do Greater Works Than What Christ Did – John 14:12

20. Can Ask for Anything in the Name of Jesus Christ – John 14:13-14

21. Has the Mind of Christ – 1 Corinthians 2:16

22. Knows All Things – 1 John 2:20

23. Knows the Truth and is Free – John 8:31-32

24. Anointed & Taught by the Anointing – 1 John 2:27

25. Has Access to the Nine Gifts of the Holy Spirit
    – 1 Corinthians 12:7-11

26. Is More Than a Conqueror – Romans 8:32

27. Wears God's Armor – Romans 13:12; Ephesians 6:10-17

28. Fights With God's Sword of the Spirit, which is the Word of
    God – Ephesians 6:17; Hebrews 4:12

29. Has the Same Faith as Jesus – Acts 3:16; 2 Corinthians 13:5;
    Galatians 2:20; Galatians 3:22-25; Ephesians 3:12

30. Has the Faith to Overcome the World- 1 John 5:4

31. Complete (No Deficiency) in Christ – Colossians 2:9-10

32. Perfected (Fully Developed) – Hebrews 10:14

33. Unblameable "Faultless" (No Charges Can Brought Against
    You) – Romans 8:31-34; Colossians 1:22

34. Unreprovable "Blameless" (Free from Any Legal Charges)
    – Colossians 1:22

35. Wise – 1 Corinthians 1:30; Colossians 2:3

36. Sanctified (Set Apart) – 1 Corinthians 1:2; 1 Corinthians 6:11; Hebrews 10:14; Jude 1:1

37. Redeemed (Full Price Paid for Our Freedom) – Galatians 3:13; 1 Peter 1:18-19

38. Holy – Ephesians 4:24

39. Righteous (In Right Standing with God) – 2 Corinthians 5:21; Philippians 3:9

40. Cannot Sin – 1 John 3:9

41. Can Eat of the Tree of Life – Revelation 22:14

42. Can Drink of the Water of Life Freely – John 4:13-14; Revelation 22:17

43. Has Rivers of Living Water Flowing Out of his Belly (Holy Spirit) – John 7:37-39

44. Can Go Boldly Before the Throne of Grace – Hebrews 4:16

45. Dwells in the Secret Place – Psalm 91:1-2

46. Can Go into the Holy of Holies – Hebrews 10:19-22

47. Has the Nine Fruits of the Spirit – Galatians 5:22-25

48. Lives in the Kingdom of God – Luke 17:20-21

49. Is a King unto God – Revelation 1:5-6; Revelation 5:9-10

50. Is a Holy & Royal Priest unto God – 1 Peter 2:4-5; 1 Peter 2:9

51. Has All things that Pertain to Life and Godliness through the Knowledge of His Divine Power – 1 Peter 1:3

52. Partakes of the Divine Nature – 1 Peter 1:4

53. Has No Curse – Galatians 3:10-13

54. Blessed with the Blessings of Abraham- Galatians 3:8-14

55. Has Riches in Glory in Christ Jesus (Prosperous) – Philippians 4:19

56. Has the Power to Get Wealth – Deuteronomy 8:18

57. Seated in Heavenly Places with Christ Jesus – Ephesians 2:4-6

58. Healthy (Is Already Healed) – 1 Peter 2:24

59. Strong In the Lord – Ephesians 6:10; Philippians 4:13

60. Has no Fear – 1 John 4:18

61. Bold – Acts 4:13; Ephesians 3:12; Hebrews 10:19-20; 1 John 4:17

62. Triumphant – 1 Corinthians 2:14

63. Has Dominion Over All Principalities and Powers – Ephesians 1:19-23; Colossians 2:9-10

64. Has the Inheritance of Christ – Ephesians 1:11; Hebrews 9:15; Ephesians 1:17-18; 1 Peter 1:3-5

65. Is In Christ – 1 Corinthians 1:30; 2 Corinthians 5:17; Ephesians 1:3; Ephesians 2:6

66. Christ is in You – Colossians 1:27

67. Has all of the Precious Promises of God – 2 Peter 1:3-4

We highly encourage you to look up each of the verses listed and let the Word of God change you from *"glory to glory."* You can also search the Scriptures, find more promises, and claim them in Christ. The riches of Christ are unsearchable, and it staggers the natural mind to think of all Christ has done for us.

> ### Ephesians 3:8 (KJV)
> *8 Unto me, who am less than the least of all saints, is this grace given, that I should preach among the Gentiles **the unsearchable riches of Christ;***

The unsearchable riches of Christ are found in your spirit, and as you realize this, they can be experienced in your soul and body. The riches of Christ, however, can only be experienced in your soul and body through faith. Faith is the secret to inheriting the promises of God. Faith allows you to see into the *Realm of the Spirit* and pull what you already have in your spirit into this life. Faith is not asking God to do anything, but faith believes and receives the finished work of Christ.

Your spiritual eyes are opened when you grasp what is in your spirit as a born-again believer. Once your eyes are opened to who you are in

Christ, you can manifest what you see with your spiritual eyes into the natural world. As you grow in the knowledge of Christ, you will learn how to renew your mind as your soul prospers in the things of God. Through this understanding, you will see who you are in the spirit, awaken your soul, and experience God's power in your body as the Spirit of the Lord quickens you.

When your heart discovers what you have in Christ in your spirit, you will sell everything you have to gain the Kingdom of God. This is why Jesus said that where a man's treasure is, there will their heart be also. Your spirit man is filled with God's fullness and is waiting for you to let out what is in your spirit through your soul and body. As you learn to live out of your spirit, you will experience the realities of Heaven on Earth in your soul and body. As we conclude this chapter, take the time to meditate with thanksgiving on what Christ has done for you and who you are in the *Realm of the Spirit.*

TO SUCCEED IN THE CHRISTIAN LIFE, YOU MUST LEARN TO LIVE OUT OF YOUR SPIRIT!

CHAPTER 5

PUT ON THE NEW MAN

Your newly created born-again spirit is what the Bible calls the *New Man*. Your *New Man* was created in the exact image of Christ and can be found, commune, and live with God in the *Realm of the Spirit.* Putting on the *New Man* is something we must do daily with the help of the Holy Spirit. As believers, it is your responsibility, not God's, as to how much of the *New Man* you want to experience in this life. In this chapter, we will teach you how to put on the *New Man* by the power of God and how to put off the Old Man.

A paradigm shift must take place in your thinking when it comes to putting on the *New Man.* Living out of the reality of the *New Man* is different than obeying the Old Testament Law. In the Old Testament, the Jews were required to obey a set of Laws given by God through Moses, but they could never be made holy in their hearts, and their sins were never fully dealt with. This is why the High Priest had to make yearly offerings for sins.

Hebrews 9:7-10 (KJV)

*7 But into the second went the high priest alone once every year, not without blood, which he offered for himself, and for the errors of the people: 8 **The Holy Ghost this signifying, that the way into the holiest of all was not yet made manifest, while as the first tabernacle was yet standing: 9 Which was a figure for the time then present, in which were offered both gifts and sacrifices, that could not make him that did the service perfect, as pertaining to the conscience;** 10 Which stood only in meats and drinks, and divers washings, and carnal ordinances, imposed on them until the time of reformation.*

As a Christian, you must put off the Old Man, who was created in the fallen image of Adam, and put on the *New Man*, who is created in the image of Christ. The way you put on the *New Man* is first to acknowledge and recognize the *New Man* is already in you. ***The New Man is the NEW YOU.*** You were made to be like Christ in the *Realm of the Spirit* when you were born again. You are not trying to please God; your *New Man* already pleases God. You are not trying to be holy; your *New Man* is holy and cannot sin. Your *New Man* is healthy and prosperous and sits in *Heavenly Places* in Christ Jesus. God considers your Old Man dead, and so should you.

Colossians 3:1-4 (KJV)

*1 **If ye then be risen with Christ, seek those things which are above, where Christ sitteth on the right hand of God.** 2 Set your affection on things above, not on things on the earth. 3 **For ye are dead, and your life is hid with Christ in***

> *God. 4 When Christ, who is our life, shall appear, then shall ye also appear with him in glory.*

The Old Testament Law was set up in such a way that the Jews were trying to please God by what they did or didn't do. This is what we call the works of The Law, and it is sad to say, but many Christians still live this way when they don't have to. When people live by works and not by the grace of God in what He accomplished for us, they are always trying to please God by what they do or don't do. True Christianity is not trying to please God through your works but accepting what Jesus did for you on the Cross and Resurrection.

Misunderstanding comes when people say, what must I do if God already did everything and made me holy? Do I do nothing if God already did everything? What must I do to be saved? Can I continue in sin and still be saved? Is there anything required of me in the message of the Gospel? These are all important questions that need to be answered.

An unrenewed mind will never understand the secret we are about to reveal. The truth is there was nothing you could do to be saved, be healed, go to Heaven, or be holy. God did everything for us in Christ, and His solution to the problem of fallen man was to recreate their dead spirit and make them a *New Man*. To receive this *New Man*, you must believe that God rose Jesus from the dead and confess Him as your Lord.

> **Romans 10:8-11 (KJV)**
> *8 But what saith it? The word is nigh thee, even in thy mouth, and in thy heart: that is, the word of faith, which we preach;*
> *9 **That if thou shalt confess with thy mouth the Lord Jesus, and shalt believe in thine heart that God hath raised him***

from the dead, thou shalt be saved. 10 For with the heart man believeth unto righteousness; and with the mouth confession is made unto salvation. 11 For the scripture saith, Whosoever believeth on him shall not be ashamed.

One could say all I have to do is believe that God raised Jesus from the dead and confess with my mouth the Lord Jesus, and I am saved. This statement is true, but you must understand what happens with this decision and confession. If someone truly makes Jesus their Lord, they submit and adhere to everything He says and obey all His commands. Jesus said: *"Why do you call me Lord, Lord, and do not the things I say?"* (Luke 6:46) A change will occur inside them when God is creating the *New Man* within them and purifying their conscience. God gives the newly saved born-again believer a new heart and a new spirit, thus changing them from the inside out.

> *Ezekiel 36:26a (KJV)*
> *26 A new heart also will I give you, and a new spirit will I put within you:*...

The newly created Christian recognizes something has changed inside them. They may still experience sickness in their body and trouble in their soul, but at the same time, they realize something happened to them deep within themselves. What happened was God came inside of them, created them as a son of God, and made them in the exact image of Christ. The rest of their Christian experience is to discover what God did for them, in them, and how they should live the rest of their lives by the power of being a son of God as a *New Man*.

Through revelation, everything changes when you discover the *New Man* and who you are in Christ. Now, with as great a revelation as this is, we must understand that our bodies and souls were not made new when we accepted Christ as our Lord. God expects us from this point forward to walk out what He put inside us. Christianity becomes a matter of allowing the *New Man* to live in your body and soul by the Spirit of the Lord. The Bible calls this putting on the *New Man*. In our soul and body, we put on what God put in us: Christ in you, your hope of Glory. You have to settle into the reality of being made new on the inside, which changes everything.

> *Colossians 1:27 (KJV)*
> *27 To whom God would make known what is the riches of the glory of this mystery among the Gentiles; **which is Christ in you, the hope of glory:***

PUT OFF & PUT ON

In light of the truth of you being a *New Man* in Christ, God expects you to put off the Old Man and walk in the newness of life. Those who put off the Old Man and put on the *New Man* show that Jesus is their Lord; they know God, and their salvation experience was genuine. Jesus will never say to the Christian who puts on the *New Man* that He doesn't know them. Jesus will only say to false believers who walk after the old sinful nature that He ***NEVER*** knew them. Putting on the *New Man* is how we prove we know God and are doing the will of God.

> *Matthew 7:21-23 (KJV)*
> *21 **Not every one that saith unto me, Lord, Lord, shall enter into the kingdom of heaven; but he that doeth the***

will of my Father which is in heaven. *22 Many will say to me in that day, Lord, Lord, have we not prophesied in thy name? and in thy name have cast out devils? and in thy name done many wonderful works? 23* **And then will I profess unto them, I never knew you: depart from me, ye that work iniquity.**

The way you put off the Old Man is to stop doing the ways of the Old Man. The Old Man behaves one way, and the *New Man*, who was created in Christ, behaves another way. Another way of saying putting off the Old Man is saying repentance. Repentance has to do with a change of thinking and acting. If someone says they are sorry for something but keep doing what they say they repented of, they haven't changed. A changed person acts differently than they used to. When referring to becoming a *New Man* in Christ, a changed person with a newly created born-again spirit will want to walk in the newness of life.

Ephesians 4:20-32 (KJV)
20 **But ye have not so learned Christ;** *21 If so be that ye have heard him, and have been taught by him, as the truth is in Jesus: 22* **That ye put off concerning the former conversation the old man, which is corrupt according to the deceitful lusts;** *23 And be renewed in the spirit of your mind; 24* **And that ye put on the new man, which after God is created in righteousness and true holiness.** *25* **Wherefore putting away** *lying, speak every man truth with his neighbour: for we are members one of another. 26 Be ye angry, and sin not: let not the sun go down upon your wrath: 27 Neither give place to the devil. 28 Let him that stole steal*

no more: but rather let him labour, working with his hands the thing which is good, that he may have to give to him that needeth. 29 Let no corrupt communication proceed out of your mouth, but that which is good to the use of edifying, that it may minister grace unto the hearers. 30 And grieve not the holy Spirit of God, whereby ye are sealed unto the day of redemption. 31 **Let all bitterness, and wrath, and anger, and clamour, and evil speaking, be put away from you, with all malice: 32 And be ye kind one to another, tenderhearted, forgiving one another, even as God for Christ's sake hath forgiven you.**

Your newly created spirit man within you hates evil and loves righteousness. Your *New Man* loves the truth and doing what is right before God. The *New Man* has a clean conscience and never wants to do anything to violate the Laws of God that are written on their heart. Once you understand who your *New Man* is, you allow your *New Man* to come out as you put off the Old Man and put on the *New Man*. You are not trying to be anything but believing by faith that God made you NEW.

> ***2 Corinthians 5:17 (KJV)***
> **17 Therefore if any man be in Christ, he is a new creature: old things are passed away; behold, all things are become new.**

Again, the way you put on the *New Man* is simply seeing the *"New You"* in the *Realm of the Spirit* and imitating Christ. You think, say, and do what you see in the Word of God about who you are, created in Christ's image. Quit doing evil and imitate Christ. The Bible describes putting off the Old Man by putting him to death. Jesus said it this way, "Take up your cross, deny yourself, and follow me." (Matthew 16:24)

> ### Colossians 3:5-14 (KJV)
>
> **5 Mortify therefore your members which are upon the earth; fornication, uncleanness, inordinate affection, evil concupiscence, and covetousness, which is idolatry**: 6 For which things' sake the wrath of God cometh on the children of disobedience: 7 In the which ye also walked some time, when ye lived in them. 8 **But now ye also put off all these; anger, wrath, malice, blasphemy, filthy communication out of your mouth. 9 Lie not one to another, seeing that ye have put off the old man with his deeds; 10 And have put on the new man, which is renewed in knowledge after the image of him that created him:** 11 Where there is neither Greek nor Jew, circumcision nor uncircumcision, Barbarian, Scythian, bond nor free: but Christ is all, and in all. 12 **Put on therefore, as the elect of God, holy and beloved, bowels of mercies, kindness, humbleness of mind, meekness, longsuffering;** 13 Forbearing one another, and forgiving one another, if any man have a quarrel against any: even as Christ forgave you, so also do ye. 14 And above all these things put on charity, which is the bond of perfectness.

You are not trying to become holy or perfect. **Your New Man is HOLY and PERFECT.** Allow Jesus, through the Holy Spirit, to live His life through you. This is called walking after the Spirit and not after the flesh. Another way to say walk in the Spirit is to put on the *New Man*. If you walk in the Spirit by putting on the *New Man*, you will not fulfill the lusts of the flesh.

> ***Galatians 5:16-25 (KJV)***
>
> *16* ***This I say then, Walk in the Spirit, and ye shall not fulfil the lust of the flesh.*** *17 For the flesh lusteth against the Spirit, and the Spirit against the flesh: and these are contrary the one to the other: so that ye cannot do the things that ye would. 18 But if ye be led of the Spirit, ye are not under the law. 19* ***Now the works of the flesh are manifest, which are these; Adultery, fornication, uncleanness, lasciviousness, 20 Idolatry, witchcraft, hatred, variance, emulations, wrath, strife, seditions, heresies, 21 Envyings, murders, drunkenness, revellings, and such like:*** *of the which I tell you before, as I have also told you in time past, that they which do such things shall not inherit the kingdom of God. 22* ***But the fruit of the Spirit is love, joy, peace, longsuffering, gentleness, goodness, faith, 23 Meekness, temperance:*** *against such there is no law. 24* ***And they that are Christ's have crucified the flesh with the affections and lusts. 25 If we live in the Spirit, let us also walk in the Spirit.***

Walking in the Spirit and putting on the *New Man* is not the works of the Law. Walking in the Spirit allows the finished work of Christ in the *New Man* to be expressed and lived out in your daily life. Living by the works of the Law would be someone trying to be holy by their works and not by accepting what Christ did for them. We are only righteous before God because we have been created in the likeness of Jesus in our *New Man*.

Philippians 3:8-11 (KJV)

*8 Yea doubtless, and I count all things but loss for the excellency of the knowledge of Christ Jesus my Lord: for whom I have suffered the loss of all things, and do count them but dung, that I may win Christ, 9 **And be found in him, not having mine own righteousness, which is of the law, but that which is through the faith of Christ, the righteousness which is of God by faith:** 10 That I may know him, and the power of his resurrection, and the fellowship of his sufferings, being made conformable unto his death; 11 If by any means I might attain unto the resurrection of the dead.*

PUT ON THE FULL ARMOR OF GOD

The armor of God is a mystery found in the Word of God that is sometimes misunderstood. Some ministers have said that the armor of God is likened to the armor the Roman soldiers used to wear. We don't know about you, but we don't want to fight the devil wearing Roman armor. The armor of God is precisely that: It's God's armor, and His armor is Heavenly. The armor of God is unique, Divine, powerful, and not of any human origin.

To understand the armor of God, you must understand the *New Man*. The *New Man* was created in Christ's likeness, and only the armor of God fits the *New Man*. The *New Man* is fully equipped and wearing the whole armor of God; however, we have to put on the armor of God to protect our bodies and souls. The armor of God is not automatically put on your body and soul when you become a Christian. You are responsible for putting on the armor of God through the power of the Holy Spirit.

The first mention of the armor of God is found in the Old Testament. The armor of God is the same armor we wear, which is why we would never say the armor of God is likened to a Roman soldier's armor. God's armor existed before the Romans were ever a nation.

> **Isaiah 59:16-17 (KJV)**
> *16 And he saw that there was no man, and wondered that there was no intercessor: therefore his arm brought salvation unto him; and his righteousness, it sustained him.*
> *17* **For he put on righteousness as a breastplate, and an helmet of salvation upon his head; and he put on the garments of vengeance for clothing, and was clad with zeal as a cloak.**

In the New Testament, we can see that we are privileged to wear the same armor that God wears. God fights our enemies with and for us and lets us wear His Holy and magnificent armor.

> **Ephesians 6:10-17 (KJV)**
> *10 Finally, my brethren, be strong in the Lord, and in the power of his might. 11* **Put on the whole armour of God, that ye may be able to stand against the wiles of the devil.**
> *12 For we wrestle not against flesh and blood, but against principalities, against powers, against the rulers of the darkness of this world, against spiritual wickedness in high places. 13* **Wherefore take unto you the whole armour of God, that ye may be able to withstand in the evil day, and having done all, to stand. 14 Stand therefore, having your loins girt about with truth, and having on the breastplate of righteousness; 15 And your feet shod with the**

preparation of the gospel of peace; 16 Above all, taking the shield of faith, wherewith ye shall be able to quench all the fiery darts of the wicked. 17 And take the helmet of salvation, and the sword of the Spirit, which is the word of God:

There is a powerful hidden mystery in the armor of God, and you must know what you are looking for to find it. Let's read a passage of Scripture together found in the Book of Romans and reveal the mystery of wearing God's armor.

Romans 13:12 (KJV)

*12 The night is far spent, the day is at hand: let us therefore cast off the works of darkness, **and let us put on the armour of light.***

This passage of Scripture describes the armor of God as being light, which we have to put on. Just like we put off the Old Man and put on the *New Man*, we put off the works of darkness and put on the armor of light. The following passage of Scripture in Romans 13 reveals the mystery of God's armor.

Romans 13:14 (KJV)

*14 **But put ye on the Lord Jesus Christ, and make not provision for the flesh, to fulfil the lusts thereof.***

The mystery of the armor of God is that we wear the Lord Jesus Christ Himself. The Lord Jesus Christ is our armor, which means He is the One who protects us against any enemy attack. So, when you bring all of the truths found in this chapter together, as you put on the *New Man*, you are putting on God's armor of light, and when you put on the armor of God, you are putting on Christ Himself. When you put on the *New Man*, you put on the Lord Jesus Christ. When you put on the *New Man*, the enemy only sees Christ fighting him.

We have the privilege of allowing Christ to live in us, on us, and through us. This is precisely how Jesus was living with the Father through the power of the Holy Spirit. Jesus said, if you have seen me, you've seen the Father. Jesus was wearing the armor of God, which was the Father Himself. When anyone, including the enemy, saw Jesus, they saw the Father.

> ### John 14:9 (KJV)
> *9 Jesus saith unto him, Have I been so long time with you, and yet hast thou not known me, Philip?* **he that hath seen me hath seen the Father; and how sayest thou then, Show us the Father?**

In conclusion, you are a *New Man* once you make Jesus your Lord, and it is your Divine privilege and responsibility to put on the Lord Jesus Christ. As you put on the Lord Jesus Christ, you are putting on the armor of God. You are no ordinary person; you are a Divine, newly created being wearing the Heavenly armor of God. You now have the Divine mandate, in the New Covenant, to put off the Old Man and put on the *New Man,* which was made in the very image of Christ. It is now time to fight the enemies of God as the mighty soldier you were created to be as you put on the *New Man* wearing the armor of God.

GOD ESTABLISHED THE NEW COVENANT FOR THE NEW MAN!

CHAPTER 6

SPIRITUAL AUTHORITY

When believers mature and awaken to the revelation of their full authority and potential in Christ as a born-again son, they are ready to take spiritual dominion on the Earth. Their positional authority in Christ empowers them to take dominion over the enemies of God and elements of the world. The believer's authority far exceeds all demonic, fallen angels, and man-made authority. Believers are granted spiritual authority in this life and throughout eternity once they accept Jesus as their Lord. Every believer's spirit is currently seated in Heavenly Places whether they know it or not, but this authority is only known through revelation and lived out as their minds are renewed to the Word of God.

When Jesus died, was buried and rose again, He was seated at the right hand of the Father and given a Name above every other name. Jesus told His disciples before His ascension that **ALL** power (authority) in Heaven and Earth was given to Him.

Matthew 28:18 (KJV)

*18 And Jesus came and spake unto them, saying, **All power is given unto me in heaven and in earth.***

This meant that Jesus didn't have all power and authority before His resurrection. Jesus had all authority in Heaven before creation but didn't have all authority on the Earth, because when Jesus created the Earth, He gave authority to Adam to take dominion over the Earth. Adam was made a little lower than the angels at the beginning of creation, and his rule and dominion were over the Earth.

Psalm 8:4-8 (KJV)

*4 What is man, that thou art mindful of him? and the son of man, that thou visitest him? 5 **For thou hast made him a little lower than the angels, and hast crowned him with glory and honour. 6 Thou madest him to have dominion over the works of thy hands; thou hast put all things under his feet:** 7 All sheep and oxen, yea, and the beasts of the field; 8 The fowl of the air, and the fish of the sea, and whatsoever passeth through the paths of the seas.*

It also says in the Book of Psalms that God gave the Earth to the children of men, but the Heavens are the Lord's.

Psalm 115:15-16 (KJV)

*15 Ye are blessed of the Lord which made heaven and earth. 16 **The heaven, even the heavens, are the Lord's: but the earth hath he given to the children of men.***

In one act of disobedience to God, Adam relinquished his authority over the Earth to the devil when he ate of the Tree of the Knowledge of Good and Evil. This act of disobedience brought in death, and the devil also gained control over hell, where souls went after they died. Now you know why Jesus had to be born as a man and die as a man. He had to be born as a man and go into the depths of hell by dying on a cross to take back the positional authority Adam gave to the devil.

When Jesus died, went to hell, and rose again, He took back all authority from the devil who had control over the keys of hell and death.

Revelation 1:18 (KJV)

*18 I am he that liveth, and was dead; and, behold, I am alive for evermore, Amen; **and have the keys of hell and of death.***

The fear of death kept people in bondage to the devil.

Hebrews 2:14-15 (KJV)

*14 Forasmuch then as the children are partakers of flesh and blood, he also himself likewise took part of the same; **that through death he might destroy him that had the power of death, that is, the devil; 15 And deliver them who through fear of death were all their lifetime subject to bondage.***

FULL AUTHORITY

Once Jesus rose from the dead, He had full authority over the Earth, not just Heaven. Now, anyone who believed Jesus rose from the dead and confessed Him as Lord would be saved.

Romans 10:8-11 (KJV)

*8 But what saith it? The word is nigh thee, even in thy mouth, and in thy heart: that is, the word of faith, which we preach; 9 **That if thou*** *shalt confess with thy mouth the Lord Jesus, and shalt believe in thine heart that God hath raised him from the dead, thou shalt be saved. 10 For with the heart man believeth unto righteousness; and with the mouth confession is made unto salvation. 11 For the scripture saith, Whosoever believeth on him shall not be ashamed.*

When people become Christians, they also have the Divine right to be a son of God.

John 1:12 (KJV)
12 But as many as received him, to them gave he power to become the sons of God, even to them that believe on his name:

Being a son of God makes you a joint heir with Christ, and this is where your authority as a believer comes from.

Romans 8:17 (KJV)
17 And if children, then heirs; heirs of God, and joint-heirs with Christ; if so be that we suffer with him, that we may be also glorified together.

As newly created sons of God, the Bible says that believers are in Christ, and Christ is in them. The fact that you are found in Christ and He is in you establishes your authority. You have no authority without Christ, but you can exercise His authority by putting on Christ as a believer.

Galatians 3:27-29 (KJV)
27 For as many of you as have been baptized into Christ have put on Christ. 28 There is neither Jew nor Greek, there is neither bond nor free, there is neither male nor female: for ye are all one in Christ

*Jesus. 29 **And if ye be Christ's, then are ye Abraham's seed, and heirs according to the promise.***

EXERCISING YOUR AUTHORITY

You exercise your authority in Christ by using the Name of Jesus Christ of Nazareth. When you command a devil to leave in the Name of Jesus Christ, it has to go because of your authority in Christ. When you use the Name of Jesus, you are using your God-given right as a son of God to take authority over sicknesses, diseases, demons, fallen angels, and even the elements of this world.

> ### John 14:13-14 (KJV)
> *13 **And whatsoever ye shall ask in my name, that will I do**, that the Father may be glorified in the Son. 14 **If ye shall ask any thing in my name, I will do it.***

In the Book of Acts, the Apostles used their authority to heal people in the Name of Jesus Christ of Nazareth. When they used the Name of Jesus, they used their Divine right as a son of God, found only in Christ. The Apostle Peter healed the lame man in Acts Chapter 3 using the Name of Jesus.

> ### Acts 3:6 (KJV)
> *6 Then Peter said, Silver and gold have I none; but such as I have give I thee: **In the name of Jesus Christ of Nazareth rise up and walk.***

Acts 3:16 (KJV)

*16 **And his name through faith in his name hath made this man strong,** whom ye see and know: yea, the faith which is by him hath given him this perfect soundness in the presence of you all.*

In Acts Chapter 4, the Apostle Peter said there was no other Name under Heaven given among men, whereby we must be saved.

Acts 4:12 (KJV)

*12 Neither is there salvation in any other: **for there is none other name under heaven given among men, whereby we must be saved.***

The Apostles did many miracles with their newfound authority in Christ. They operated in the supernatural and cast out demons in the Name of Jesus Christ of Nazareth. The authority of Jesus was operating in the Church, and they were shaking the gates of hell while turning the world upside down. Using the authority they were given in Christ, these newly born-again sons of God changed nations and turned many away from the works of darkness into the children of light.

To understand how these early disciples did such mighty acts, we must know what they knew. Remember, these early disciples walked with Jesus for close to three years. Jesus also gave them revelational knowledge of what He accomplished when He rose from the dead. These early disciples understood from the mouth of Christ who they were. Jesus revealed to His early disciples the authority and power of their new birth as sons of God.

SEATED IN HEAVENLY PLACES

When Adam was created, his position was below the angels, but believers in Christ are now positioned above the angels and seated next to Christ on His Throne. The Bible even says that we will judge angels. It also says that saints are going to judge the world. You cannot judge something that is above you. Newly created sons of God are positioned above fallen man, demons, fallen angels, and angels because we are in Christ and one with Him.

> *1 Corinthians 6:2-3 (KJV)*
> *2 **Do ye not know that the saints shall judge the world?** and if the world shall be judged by you, are ye unworthy to judge the smallest matters? 3 **Know ye not that we shall judge angels?** how much more things that pertain to this life?*

Having authority and exercising judgment is what it means to be seated in Heavenly Places.

> *Ephesians 2:6 (KJV)*
> *6 **And hath raised us up together, and made us sit together in heavenly places in Christ Jesus:***

As the Bride of Christ, we have authority because the ONE we are married to has ALL authority. We are sons of God; the Father Himself gives us authority because we are joined as ONE with His Son. We are also predestined to walk in authority in the age to come as the Bride of Christ.

Revelation 21:2 (KJV)
2 And I John saw the holy city, new Jerusalem, coming down from God out of heaven, prepared as a bride adorned for her husband.

Ephesians 5:30-32 (KJV)
*30 For we are members of his body, of his flesh, and of his bones. 31 For this cause shall a man leave his father and mother, and shall be joined unto his wife, **and they two shall be one flesh. 32 This is a great mystery: but I speak concerning Christ and the church.***

Below is the order of *Spiritual Rankings* from the original creation to what we now have in Christ. This ranking order will help you understand your position after accepting Jesus as your Lord. You were not reinstated to Adam's original authority when you were born again; you were given more authority and seated above all creation next to Christ. Born again, sons of God in Christ are the highest spiritual beings in Authority & Power under the Father and Holy Spirit and over all of creation. The Father, the Holy Spirit, and Jesus are the only *Spiritual Beings* greater than you. New Testament believers are created in the exact likeness of Jesus and share in His Kingdom, Throne, Authority, and Power. All of creation is waiting for the sons of God to be revealed.

Romans 8:19 (KJV)
*19 **For the earnest expectation of the creature waiteth for the manifestation of the sons of God.***

SPIRITUAL RANKINGS

ORIGINAL CREATION

- Father – (Full Authority & Power over Heaven/Creation)

- Holy Spirit – (Full Authority & Power over Heaven/Creation)

- Jesus (Son of God) – (Full Authority & Power over Heaven/Creation)

- Angels (Servants) – (Limited Authority & Power over Heaven/Creation)

- Adam/Mankind (sons of God) – (Full Authority & Power over the Earth)

- Satan/Fallen Angels (Enemies) – (No Authority or Power over Heaven/Creation) – Some angels fell away before creation. Other angels, known as sons of God in Genesis 6, fell away after the fall of Adam.

AFTER THE FALL

- Father – (Full Authority & Power over Heaven/Creation)

- Holy Spirit – (Full Authority & Power over Heaven/Creation)

- Jesus (Son of God) – (Full Authority & Power over Heaven/Creation)

- Angels (Servants) – (Limited Authority & Power over Heaven/Creation)

- Satan/Fallen Angels/Demons (Oppressors/Enemies) – (Limited Authority & Power over the Earth) – Going to the Lake of Fire

- Fallen Mankind (Captives) – (No Spiritual Authority & Limited Power over the Earth) – Going to Tormenting Hell or Abraham's Bosom

SECRET MISSION OF CHRIST

- Father – (Full Authority & Power over Heaven/Creation)

- Holy Spirit – (Full Authority & Power over Heaven/Creation)

- Angels (Servants) – (Limited Authority & Power over Heaven/Creation)

- Jesus/Second Adam (Liberator/Conqueror) – (Limited Authority & Power over the Earth) – Went to Abraham's Bosom

- Satan/Fallen Angels/Demons (Oppressors/Enemies) – (Limited Authority & Power over the Earth) – Going to the Lake of Fire

- Fallen Mankind (Captives) – (Limited Spiritual Authority & Power over the Earth) – Going to Tormenting Hell or Abraham's Bosom

AFTER THE RESURRECTION

- Father – (Full Authority & Power over Heaven/Creation)

- Holy Spirit – (Full Authority & Power over Heaven/Creation)

- Jesus/Church (Sons of God/New Creations) (Liberators) – (All Authority & Power over Heaven/Creation)

- Angels (Servants) – (Limited Authority & Power over Heaven/Creation)

- Satan/Fallen Angels/Demons (Oppressors/Enemies) – (No Authority or Power over the Earth) – Going to the Lake of Fire

- Fallen Mankind (Captives) – (No Spiritual Authority & Limited Power over the Earth) – Going to Tormenting Hell

END OF THE AGE

- Father – (Full Authority & Power over Heaven/Creation)

- Holy Spirit – (Full Authority & Power over Heaven/Creation)

- Jesus/Church (Sons of God/New Creations) (Kings & Priests) – (Full Authority & Power over Heaven/Creation)

- Angels (Servants) – (Limited Authority & Power over Heaven/Creation)

- Satan/Fallen Angels/Demons (Enemies) – Lake of Fire (No Authority or Power)

- Fallen Mankind (Enemies) – Lake of Fire (No Authority or Power)

When you fully know who Jesus created you to be as a son of God, you will never be the same. Once you understand you are a New Creation in Christ, your mind will begin to be renewed to your authority and power. As you renew your mind to these Divine truths and acknowledge who you are in Christ, you will go from glory to glory while you learn to exercise your authority in Christ.

It is essential to realize that the enemy does not want you to know who you are in Christ and tries to keep believers blinded to their God-given authority. Once you know your authority and learn how to use the Name of Jesus with your faith, you are no longer a slave under the dominion of the devil. The devil and all of his cohorts are forced to obey your God-given authority.

Christians have more authority than angels, demons, fallen angels, fallen humankind, animals, and all of creation. Jesus knew who He was and took authority everywhere He went. He commanded storms, demons, the devil, fallen angels, sickness, diseases, trees, mountains, and death to obey Him. Then, He gave His Church authority and commanded them to do the same.

> ### *Mark 16:15-20 (KJV)*
> *15 And he said unto them, Go ye into all the world, and preach the gospel to every creature. 16 He that believeth and is baptized shall be saved; but he that believeth not shall be damned. 17 **And these signs shall follow them that believe; In my name shall they cast out devils; they shall speak with new tongues; 18 They shall take up serpents; and if they drink any deadly thing, it shall not hurt them; they shall lay hands on the sick, and they shall recover.** 19 So then after the Lord had spoken unto them, he was received up into heaven, and sat on the right hand of God. 20 And they went forth, and preached every where, **the Lord working with them, and confirming the word with signs following. Amen.***

ACKNOWLEDGED AUTHORITY

Your spiritual authority must be acknowledged before exercising it with your faith. The eyes of your understanding must be enlightened to know who you are and the hope of your calling. This authority will become your new reality as you renew your mind. As you walk in your Heavenly authority in Christ, you will exercise your faith, and mountains will move as you turn the world upside down through the power of the Gospel. Anyone who walks in faith knows the authority they have in Christ. You cannot walk in commanding faith if you don't walk in commanding authority. We see this truth in how Jesus responded to the Roman Centurion, who understood authority.

Luke 7:2-10 (KJV)

*2 And a certain centurion's servant, who was dear unto him, was sick, and ready to die. 3 And when he heard of Jesus, he sent unto him the elders of the Jews, beseeching him that he would come and heal his servant. 4 And when they came to Jesus, they besought him instantly, saying, That he was worthy for whom he should do this: 5 For he loveth our nation, and he hath built us a synagogue. 6 Then Jesus went with them. And when he was now not far from the house, the centurion sent friends to him, saying unto him, Lord, trouble not thyself: for I am not worthy that thou shouldest enter under my roof: 7 Wherefore neither thought I myself worthy to come unto thee: but say in a word, and my servant shall be healed. 8 **For I also am a man set under authority, having under me soldiers, and I say unto one, Go, and he goeth; and to another, Come, and he cometh; and to my servant, Do this, and he doeth it.** 9 When Jesus heard these things, he marvelled at him, and turned him about, and said unto the people that followed him, **I say unto you, I have not found so great** *faith, no, not in Israel. 10 And they that were sent, returning to the house, found the servant whole that had been sick.*

Just because you have authority as a born-again son of God, it will not fully manifest until you grow into it through revelational knowledge. This revelational knowledge is only given to mature believers who renew their minds and know who they are in Christ through the Word of God. These are the ones who have done the work of reaping a harvest of the Kingdom. They understand, keep, and focus on the Word of God and thereby reap a hundredfold of their authority in Christ. When they mature in Christ, the Father grants them the ability to walk in their Divine Authority as a son of God.

Galatians 4:1-6 (KJV)
*1 Now I say, That the heir, as long as he is a child, differeth nothing from a servant, though he be lord of all; 2 **But is under tutors and governors until the time appointed of the father. 3 Even so we, when we were children, were in bondage under the elements of the world:** 4 But when the fulness of the time was come, God sent forth his Son, made of a woman, made under the law, 5 To redeem them that were under the law, that we might receive the adoption of sons. 6 And because ye are sons, God hath sent forth the Spirit of his Son into your hearts, crying, Abba, Father.*

SPIRITUAL MATURITY

Spiritual maturity takes time, effort, and commitment. The more you renew your mind, the faster you will grow up in Christ. Some Christians have attempted to exercise their authority in Christ but failed because they have not yet grown to that level. It is also important to note that

Jesus, as mature as He was, didn't walk in any miracles until He was thirty years old. When He was thirty, He had a defining moment when John the Baptist baptized Him in the Jordan River. The Father spoke over Him, saying He was His beloved Son, with whom He was well pleased. The Holy Spirit also descended upon Jesus like a dove and drove Him into the wilderness to be tested by the enemy. When Jesus passed His tests, He came out in the power of the Holy Spirit, worked miracles, and exercised His spiritual authority.

If Jesus had to pass tests before He was granted the privilege of walking in the power of the Holy Spirit, then we shall also have to pass tests before walking in our God-given authority. Passing tests is a sign you are maturing spiritually. Once you understand this, you will know the importance of being faithful and renewing your mind to the Word of God so you can pass any test the enemy may throw at you. It is up to us to grow up if we want to walk in all the authority God has given us as sons of God. Growing up is not easy, but it is eternally advantageous when we do.

In conclusion, God has given us authority as newly created, born-again sons of God, and we far outrank the enemy. It is a Divine privilege to become a son of God, be seated in Heavenly Places, and walk in the authority of the age to come. Believers in Christ will have the Eternal privilege of sharing the Throne of God as a joint heir with Christ. Those who spiritually mature in Christ can walk in their *Divine Authority* before they go to Heaven. It is up to you what you will do with your *Divine Potential!*

BORN AGAIN SONS OF GOD OUTRANK EVERY CREATED BEING IN THE UNIVERSE!

CHAPTER 7

MIND RENEWAL

O ne of the most rewarding accomplishments you will ever achieve as a believer is to renew your mind. It takes daily minute-by-minute discipline of reading the Word of God, study, meditation, confession, memorization, acknowledgment, time, focus, discipleship, preaching, teaching, praying, and spiritual warfare to renew your mind. Your mind will not renew itself, and it is your responsibility, with the help of the Holy Spirit to renew your mind to the will of God. A fully renewed mind thinks exactly like Jesus, and an unrenewed mind thinks like the devil. There is no middle ground, so the more you renew your mind to the Word of God, the more Christlike you will become. In this chapter, we will reveal secrets on how to renew your mind so you can manifest who God has created you to be in the image of Christ.

The mystery of what Christ placed inside you when you were born again is unlocked through mind renewal and Divine revelation from the Word of God. As you hear, read, and do the Word of God, your mind is renewed more and more. The power of God works with and flows through a mind that is renewed by the Word of God and thinks like Christ. One of the main reasons Christian minds are not renewed is because they don't know the Scriptures nor the power of God.

Matthew 22:29 (KJV)
29 Jesus answered and said unto them, ***Ye do err, not knowing the scriptures, nor the power of God.***

God knows who you are and hopes you will discover who you are and what He has done for you through Christ. The devil also knows who you are and hopes you won't find out. You are the only person who may or may not know who you entirely are, but God has placed this responsibility on you through mind renewal to find out who you are and what you have in Christ. Many Christians have missed their Divine Rights and privileges by not renewing their mind to God's Word. The devil will fight Christians tooth and nail to keep them in spiritual darkness with an unrenewed mind.

2 Corinthians 4:3-4 (KJV)
3 But if our gospel be hid, it is hid to them that are lost: 4 ***In whom the god of this world hath blinded the minds of them which believe not,*** *lest the light of the glorious gospel of Christ, who is the image of God, should shine unto them.*

The Bible says that we have the mind of Christ (1 Corinthians 2:16). We are also told in Philippians 2:5 (KJV) *"Let this mind be in you, which was also in Christ Jesus:"* The mind of Christ is something you were given in your spirit when you were born again, but it takes the renewing of your mind to get the mind of Christ in your natural mind. This is where His thoughts become your thoughts in every area of your life. When you renew your mind to line up with Christ's mind, your life will be transformed, and you will prove what is the good, acceptable, and perfect will of God.

> *Romans 12:2 (KJV)*
> *2 And be not conformed to this world: but be ye transformed by the renewing of your mind, that ye may prove what is that good, and acceptable, and perfect, will of God.*

Your mind is renewed to the Word of God to the degree that the Word of God dictates your daily actions and how you think, act, and live. When your mind is fully renewed, you will no longer think as the world thinks, but you will think with the holy mind of Christ in every area of your life. Jesus did not think like mere human beings think. Jesus was always Heavenly-minded, and He had faith in His Father to come through and help others and Himself with whatever they needed. Jesus had a miracle mindset that pushed through every obstacle with astounding faith. Jesus was constantly connected to His Heavenly Father and the Holy Spirit and understood that nothing was impossible with God. Jesus also taught His disciples to think the same way, which is why they went on to do miracles and great things for God.

It is important to remember that the Apostles left everything to follow Christ and to be with Him daily for nearly three years. During this time, their minds were being renewed to think like Christ. This reveals that for your mind to be renewed, you must give up many things, stay focused, and be trained by the Word of God. From the Old Testament, we know that Elisha left everyone and everything to be mentored by Elijah. Elisha picked up Elijah's mantle and walked in miracles because his mind was renewed by being around Elijah. Joshua was also a shining example of a man of God who followed Moses and renewed his mind from the Word of God to the point where God could use him to lead the children of Israel in possessing the Promised Land.

When you read the stories in the New Testament of Jesus confronting His disciples every time they were in fear, doubt, and unbelief, He was renewing their minds. We can see that after Jesus rose from the dead, He was still working on renewing their minds. Jesus successfully took tax collectors, fishermen, and ordinary men and renewed their minds because, in the Book of Acts, they went on to do more miracles than Jesus performed and even greater.

HEART WARFARE

We want to point out that mind renewal has the goal of reaping a harvest in your heart. The battle is in the mind, but the war is for your heart. As you win daily battles in your thought life through the Word of God, you allow God and His Word to plant seeds in your heart that you will reap. You must gain the victory in your mind to protect and guard your heart so God can use you to reap a harvest in His Kingdom. This is why the Bible says we have to take every thought captive to the obedience of Christ.

> *2 Corinthians 10:3-6 (KJV)*
> *3 For though we walk in the flesh, we do not war after the flesh: 4 (For the weapons of our warfare are not carnal, but mighty through God to the pulling down of strong holds;) 5 **Casting down imaginations, and every high thing that exalteth itself against the knowledge of God, and bringing into captivity every thought to the***

*obedience of Christ; 6 And having in a readiness to revenge all
disobedience, when your obedience is fulfilled.*

There are many ways to get from California to New York; however, what
you choose as a mode of transportation will determine the time it takes
you to get there. It will take someone driving a car much longer to get to
New York than someone flying on a plane. How fast you renew your
mind is up to you. Those who choose full submersion will renew their
minds much quicker, just like the Apostles did when they left everything
to follow Christ.

You may not be called to leave everything behind at this time, but that
does not mean you cannot choose to renew your mind as much as you
can every day. We know from the Scriptures that God told Joshua to
meditate on the Word of God day and night (Joshua 1:8). The Apostle
Paul told Timothy not to neglect the gift that was given to him by
prophecy but to mediate and give himself wholly to them and that if he
did, his profiting would appear to all (1 Timothy 4:14-15). We also know
that King David had great success because his delight was in the Law of
the Lord, and he meditated on God's Law day and night. King David
didn't get distracted by the counsel of the ungodly, stand in the way of
sinners, or sit in the seat of the scornful.

Psalm 1:1-3 (KJV)
*1 Blessed is the man that walketh not in the counsel of the ungodly,
nor standeth in the way of sinners, nor sitteth in the seat of the
scornful. 2 But his delight is in the law of the Lord; and in his law
doth he meditate day and night. 3 And he shall be like a tree planted
by the rivers of water, that bringeth forth his fruit in his season; his
leaf also shall not wither; and whatsoever he doeth shall prosper.*

SOWER SOWS THE WORD

In the *Sower Sows the Word* parable, Jesus revealed the mystery of reaping a harvest of the Kingdom of God. This parable mostly talks about the heart but can also be applied to mind renewal. As you study this parable, you will become aware that mind renewal and heart productivity go beyond just hearing God's Word preached. Jesus revealed in this parable that the person hearing the Word of God was responsible for reaping a hundredfold harvest of the Kingdom of God.

Four types of people are revealed in this parable of the *Sower Sows the Word*, but only one type of person experiences the privilege of reaping a harvest because the Word of God renewed their mind and transformed their heart. It is also revealed that even when a person renews their mind, they still have levels of mind renewal. Some reap thirtyfold, some reap sixtyfold, and others reap hundredfold benefits from the Kingdom of God with a productive heart and renewed mind.

Let's read what Jesus revealed to His faithful disciples in the parable of the *Sower Sows the Word* and how it can be applied to mind renewal.

Matthew 13:18-23 (KJV)
*18 Hear ye therefore the parable of the sower. 19 When any one heareth the word of the kingdom, **and understandeth it not**, then cometh the wicked one, and catcheth away that which was sown in his heart. This is he which received seed by the way side. 20 But he that received the seed into stony places, the same is he that heareth the word, and anon with joy receiveth it; 21 **Yet hath he not root in himself, but dureth for a while:** for when tribulation or persecution ariseth because of the word, by and by he is offended. 22 He also*

*that received seed among the thorns is he that heareth the word; **and the care of this world, and the deceitfulness of riches, choke the word, and he becometh unfruitful. 23 But he that received seed into the good ground is he that heareth the word, and understandeth it; which also beareth fruit, and bringeth forth, some an hundredfold, some sixty, some thirty.***

The first person who hears the Word sown in their heart has the Word of God stolen from them by a lack of understanding. The devil stole the understanding of the Word of God from them, and they were not able to see the truth of what God was trying to teach them. Jesus reveals with this first person that understanding God's Word is the first step in mind renewal and transforming your heart. An unrenewed mind doesn't understand the truth of God's Word. An unrenewed mind also thinks God's ways are foolish because it doesn't understand God and His ways.

1 Corinthians 2:14 (KJV)
*14 **But the natural man receiveth not the things of the Spirit of God: for they are foolishness unto him: neither can he know them, because they are spiritually discerned.***

The second person has an unrenewed mind because they are unwilling to stay committed to the effort and warfare to renew the mind and produce a harvest of the Kingdom of God. This type of person starts with great joy but gives up when facing tribulation and persecution because of the Word of God. This tells us that there will be opposition to mind renewal and reaping a harvest in your heart, but if you are willing to stay in the fight and never give up, your mind will be renewed. A renewed mind is committed to God and the truth no matter the opposition, obstacles, or problems they face.

The third person who fails to renew their mind starts out great and is close to receiving a harvest of the Kingdom in their heart but gets distracted with the cares of this life and the deceitfulness of riches. This type of person has a heart that will not focus long enough to receive a harvest. This tells us that for mind renewal to occur, you must stay focused long enough before seeing the fruits of your labor. Mind renewal and heart transformation do not take place overnight. It takes concentrated effort and focus over an extended period of time for the mind to be renewed and to reap a harvest of the Kingdom of God. A renewed mind is singular in focus and does not get distracted by anything or anyone.

The fourth person who renews their mind has a good heart that understands, stays committed, and remains focused on the Word of God through the long season it takes to reap a harvest. This person is faithful and has one goal: to renew their mind to think as Christ thinks and reap a harvest in their heart. They fought through difficulties and remained steadfast, and they were the ones who reaped the benefits of a renewed mind and transformed heart. History shows us that everyone who renewed their mind went on to reap a harvest in the Kingdom of God and did great exploits through the power of God. These people pleased God with their faith; nothing was impossible for them because they thought like God and inherited the precious promises of God.

WHAT ARE YOU LOOKING AT?

Whatever you look at, you will become, and the more you look at something, the more of it you will get in your life. As you spend time looking at, reading, thinking, and speaking the Word of God day and night, your mind will begin to be renewed, and you will see a transformation in your heart. King Solomon knew this principle and wrote about it in the Book of Proverbs many years before Christ came and revealed secrets to mind renewal.

> ***Proverbs 4:20-27 (KJV)***
> *20 **My son, attend to my words;** incline thine ear unto my sayings. 21 **Let them not depart from thine eyes; keep them in the midst of thine heart**. 22 For they are life unto those that find them, and health to all their flesh. 23 **Keep thy heart with all diligence; for out of it are the issues of life.** 24 Put away from thee a froward mouth, and perverse lips put far from thee. 25 **Let thine eyes look right on, and let thine eyelids look straight before thee.** 26 Ponder the path of thy feet, and let all thy ways be established. 27 Turn not to the right hand nor to the left: remove thy foot from evil.*

People who waste time in their lives away by watching mindless worldly movies, TV, news, playing video games, engaging in too much social media, and listening to godless music will never renew their minds. Mind renewal has much to do with what you look at and listen to. Watching worldly shows and listening to worldly music will make you think like the world. If you look at and read the Word of God, you will become what you read and look at with your eyes. It is also essential to fellowship with like-minded believers and listen to anointed teaching and preaching to renew your mind. If you do these things, your mind will renew faster. It takes being single-minded to become like God and being filled with the light of His knowledge.

Luke 11:34 (KJV)
*34 **The light of the body is the eye: therefore when thine eye is
single, thy whole body also is full of light;** but when thine eye is evil,
thy body also is full of darkness.*

What you look at before you go to bed and what you look at when you
wake up in the morning play an essential role in mind renewal. Whatever
you look at before you go to bed sticks with you through the night. If you
go to bed with God in your thoughts, He can talk to you while you sleep,
give you Heavenly dreams, and speak with you when you wake up. If
you fill your mind with the world, news, and garbage all day and before
you go to bed, you will miss out on many revelations from God He can
give you throughout the night. The more you look at and read the Word
of God, the more precise you will hear God speak to you. Jewish parents
learned early on to teach their children the Word of God and its effect on
them throughout the day, night, and when they woke up.

Proverbs 6:20-22 (KJV)
*20 My son, keep thy father's commandment, and forsake not the law
of thy mother: 21 Bind them continually upon thine heart, and tie
them about thy neck. 22 **When thou goest, it shall lead thee; when
thou sleepest, it shall keep thee; and when thou awakest, it shall
talk with thee.***

Below is a list of ways you can renew your mind. The more you commit
to doing this list, the faster your mind will be renewed. Remember, it is
up to you and not God to renew your mind. God has done everything He
is going to do; it is now up to us to do our part to come into alignment
with who God said we are and what we have in Christ. This list is a secret

to renewing your mind; those willing to do the work it takes to renew their mind will reap the benefits.

SECRETS TO RENEWING YOUR MIND

1. Read your Bible as much as you can

2. Stay focused on the Word of God day and night

3. Be led by the Holy Spirit what to read and study from the Word of God

4. Study your Bible – Rightly divide the Word of Truth

5. Memorize Scriptures

6. Ask God for Divine Revelation on Bible verses you don't understand

7. Obey and practice what you read from your Bible

8. Discipleship (personalized mind renewal) - Be open to spiritual fathering from anointed ministers. Be open to them challenging your wrong ways of thinking. Walk with them daily.

9. Keep your mind stayed on God all day long – Focus on God and look at Jesus and who you are in the Spirit

10. Learn to keep your mind stayed on God while you are working or doing earthly tasks

11. Practice the Presence of God all day long

12. Intently stare and gaze upon the Word of God with prolonged concentration and uninterrupted focus

13. Remove all distractions from your life and thought life

14. Separate yourself from any relationships that will not support you in coming into the image of who you are in Christ

15. Confess the Word of God – Your ears have to hear you speaking the Word of God

16. Handwrite Scriptures or type them into a Word Doc

17. Repetition, frequency, and consistency in the Word of God

18. Fully immerse yourself in the things of God

19. Go away somewhere private and seclude yourself as much as you can to spend alone time with God (No distractions – TV, phone, computer, internet and people)

20. Enter into deep meditation on the Word of God

21. Meditate on the Image of what Jesus and you look like in the Spirit

22. Specifically, meditate on all the Words of Christ, His Commands, and His parables

23. Wholly give yourself to what you are meditating on

24. Continue with intense focus on the Word of God until your harvest comes

25. Spend most of your time thinking about Christ and who He is

26. Keep your mind engaged and connected to God at all times

27. Separate yourself from anything worldly

28. Think about the price Christ paid for you

29. Acknowledge and confess that you have the mind of Christ

30. Think about you being in Christ and Christ being in you

31. Stay in constant fellowship and communion with God all day long

32. Pray that God opens the eyes of your understanding

33. Force your mind to think only on what is true, honest, just, pure, lovely, of a good report, virtue, and any praise

34. Examine all of your belief systems and challenge them with the Word of God

35. Talk to yourself rather than listen to yourself

36. Use your self-talk to speak to yourself what the Word of God says you have and who you are in the Spirit

37. Remove any distractions from your life that will take your thoughts away from God and His Word

38. Protect your eyes and ears - Don't let your eyes or ears see or hear anything that would sow seeds of contrary images and thoughts to the Word of God into your heart

39. Protect and guard your heart with all diligence

40. Be watchful and mindful of anything and everything that comes into your ears and eyes and out your mouth

41. Know that what you look at, you become

42. Know that what you listen to, you become

43. Know that what comes out of your mouth, you become

44. Regularly watch & listen to anointed preaching and teaching (Be careful who you receive from, because you will become like them)

45. Law of progressive overload. You have to constantly be doing more today than you did yesterday if you want to grow

46. Talk to other Christians about the Word of God - anointed fellowship

47. Meditate on every good thing God has done for you, and be grateful

48. Speak in tongues

49. Prophesy

50. Pray without ceasing

51. Sing spiritual songs, psalms, hymns, the Word of God, and songs of deliverance

52. Repent and forsake wicked ways and cast down unrighteous thoughts and imaginations

53. Only watch things on TV and the Internet (YouTube, Google, & social media) that are godly

54. Don't set any wicked thing before your eyes

55. Only listen to anointed Christian songs that have correct theology

56. Pull down strongholds (wrong thinking patterns) in your mind

57. Cast down imaginations that are against the thoughts of God

58. Cast down every high thing that exalts itself against the knowledge of God

59. Bring every thought captive to the obedience of Christ

60. Rebuke and bind the devil or any hindering spirit trying to take your understanding of the Word of God

61. Bind the enemy from blinding your eyes from seeing the light of the knowledge of the Glory of God in the face of Jesus Christ

DOUBLE-MINDED

A double-minded person has an unrenewed mind. On one side of their mind, they believe God has done everything through the redemption of Christ, and then on the other side of their mind, they don't believe He will do anything for them. When their experience doesn't align with what they thought was the Word of God, they change their belief systems. A double-minded person is filled with truth from the Word of God and false doctrines.

> ### *James 1:5-8 (KJV)*
> *5 If any of you lack wisdom, let him ask of God, that giveth to all men liberally, and upbraideth not; and it shall be given him. 6 But let him ask in faith, nothing wavering. For he that wavereth is like a wave of the sea driven with the wind and tossed. 7 For let not that man think that he shall receive any thing of the Lord. 8 **A double minded man is unstable in all his ways.**

No one ever promised that mind renewal would be easy, but we guarantee that anyone who renews their mind will have a better time serving God than someone who has not. The faster you renew your mind, the quicker you will inherit the promises of God. The rewards of renewing your mind far outweigh the work it takes to renew it. Once your mind is renewed and you start harvesting the Kingdom of God, you are never the same and never want to return to your old, double-minded ways.

In conclusion, mind renewal is one of your most critical spiritual accomplishments. God has done so much for us, and it is our responsibility through the leading of the Holy Spirit to do what it takes to find out what He has done and walk in it through a renewed mind. The best way to appreciate what Christ has done for you is to renew your mind. A renewed mind will give God glory on Judgment Day. Thank God we have a window of time to renew our minds and become like Christ.

THE PROMISES OF GOD ARE WAITING FOR THOSE WHO RENEW THEIR MIND!

CHAPTER 8

IMAGINATION

Your imagination is integral to your daily life, whether you know it or not. You can only see into the unseen realm and function in this world through your imagination. Your imagination also allows you to see Christ inside of you and who you are in Him through the Word of God. When you learn how to use your imagination the way God designed it to be used, you can work with the Holy Spirit to see the unseen and hope against hope as you wait on the Lord to fulfill His promises. If you can see something inside you with the spiritual eyes of your imagination, you will see it on the outside. In this chapter, we will help reveal the power of your imagination and how you can use it combined with your faith to receive answers to your prayers and discover who you are in Christ.

In your imagination, thoughts are conceived, formed, and framed in your heart like pictures or movies. You conceive within your imagination what you want to see manifested in the seen world from the unseen world. With your imagination, you can create a mental image of something not present or something you have not experienced before.

You can also use your imagination to remember past experiences. God communicates to you through your imagination in the invisible realm through visions, dreams, and trances. When the Bible says we walk by faith and not by sight, this refers to believers using their imagination combined with the Word of God to see into the unseen realm.

> *2 Corinthians 5:7 (KJV)*
> *7 (For we walk by faith, not by sight:)*

When Adam and Eve fell, mankind's imagination went dark, and humankind started using their imagination for evil. The Book of Romans says they became vain in their imaginations, and their foolish heart was darkened.

> *Romans 1:21 (KJV)*
> *21 Because that, when they knew God, they glorified him not as God, neither were thankful;* **but became vain in their imaginations, and their foolish heart was darkened.**

During Noah's time, the Bible says that the wickedness of man was great on the Earth and that every imagination of the thoughts of their heart was only evil continually. This wickedness found in their heart and imagination was the reason God flooded the Earth.

> *Genesis 6:5-7 (KJV)*
> *5 And God saw that the wickedness of man was great in the earth,* **and that every imagination of the thoughts of his heart was only evil continually.** *6 And it repented the Lord that he had made man on the earth, and it grieved him at his heart. 7* **And the Lord said, I will destroy man whom I have**

created from the face of the earth; both man, and beast, and the creeping thing, and the fowls of the air; for it repenteth me that I have made them.

TOWER OF BABEL

After the flood, humanity still used their imaginations for their own purpose, not God's will. Fallen humankind used their imagination to build a tower to reach Heaven. This went against God's mandate for man to multiply and take dominion over the Earth (Genesis 1:27-28). God came down to see the tower they were building in the land of Shinar, which became known as the Tower of Babel, and decided to confound their language so they couldn't understand each other. After this event, they were scattered abroad upon the face of the whole Earth.

> ### Genesis 11:1-9 (KJV)
> *1 And the whole earth was of one language, and of one speech. 2 And it came to pass, as they journeyed from the east, that they found a plain in the land of Shinar; and they dwelt there. 3 And they said one to another, Go to, let us make brick, and burn them thoroughly. And they had brick for stone, and slime had they for morter. 4 And they said, Go to, let us build us a city and a tower, whose top may reach unto heaven; and let us make us a name, lest we be scattered abroad upon the face of the whole earth. 5 And the Lord came down to see the city and the tower, which the children of men builded. 6 **And the Lord said, Behold, the people is one, and they have all one language; and this they begin to do: and now nothing will be restrained from them, which they have imagined to do.** 7 **Go to, let us go***

*down, and there confound their language, that they may not understand one another's speech. 8 So the Lord scattered them abroad from thence upon the face of all the earth: and they left off to build the city. 9 Therefore is the name of it called **Babel**; because **the Lord did there confound the language of all the earth:** and from thence did the Lord scatter them abroad upon the face of all the earth.*

One verse gives significant insight into the power of imagination from this passage. Verse 6 says that nothing would be restrained from them, which they imagined to do.

> *Genesis 11:6b (KJV)*
> *6 ...and now nothing will be restrained from them, which they have imagined to do.*

The Amplified Bible, Classic Edition says: *"...this is only the beginning of what they will do, and now nothing they have imagined they can do will be impossible for them."* God foresaw humanity using their imagination for evil and their own purposes. Even after God confused humankind's language, we see them, even to this day, still using their imagination to do evil and walk in ways that are contrary to the Divine life of God!

> *Ephesians 4:17-19 (KJV)*
> *17 This I say therefore, and testify in the Lord, **that ye henceforth walk not as other Gentiles walk, in the vanity of their mind,** 18 **Having the understanding darkened, being alienated from the life of God through the ignorance**

that is in them, because of the blindness of their heart: 19
Who being past feeling have given themselves over unto
lasciviousness, to work all uncleanness with greediness.

MOUNTAIN MOVING IMAGINATION

The people at the Tower of Babel were not just building a structure, but they were using their imagination to create evil. God said nothing would be impossible for them when they used their imagination. When you start using the word impossible, this is the same language Jesus used about believers speaking to mountains and working miracles.

> *Matthew 17:20 (KJV)*
> *20 And Jesus said unto them, Because of your unbelief: for verily I say unto you, If ye have faith as a grain of mustard seed, ye shall say unto this mountain, Remove hence to yonder place; and it shall remove;* **and nothing shall be impossible unto you.**

Many believers have spoken to spiritual mountains, didn't see them move, and wondered why. When the mountain didn't move, they concluded that what Jesus said was untrue. However, to fully understand how a mountain moves with your faith, you must understand the importance of your imagination. Remember, Jesus used the term *"mountain"* to symbolize anything standing in your way. You can speak to a mountain until you are blue in the face, and it will not move unless you see it moving in the imagination of your heart. Let's look at another verse in the Book of Mark where Jesus teaches about moving mountains by faith in God.

Mark 11:22-24 (KJV)

22 And Jesus answering saith unto them, Have faith in God.
23 For verily I say unto you, That whosoever shall say unto this mountain, Be thou removed, and be thou cast into the sea; and shall not doubt in his heart, but shall believe that those things which he saith shall come to pass; he shall have whatsoever he saith. *24 Therefore I say unto you, What things soever ye desire, when ye pray, believe that ye receive them, and ye shall have them.*

In this passage of Scripture, Jesus reveals a great secret about moving mountains by faith. Jesus said for you to successfully move a mountain with faith-filled words, you cannot have any doubt in your heart. We know the Bible teaches that out of the abundance of the heart, the mouth speaks, and it is in your heart where your imagination is found. You cannot have any images of doubt in your heart when speaking to a mountain and commanding it to move with your faith.

Your words have no power unless they are filled with faith, and we know faith is the substance of things hoped for, the evidence of things not seen.

Hebrews 11:1 (KJV)
*1 **Now faith is the substance of things hoped for, the evidence of things not seen.***

To fully understand how faith works, you have to understand the word hope. What is hope? Hope is an expectation with a great desire for something to manifest in your life. Biblical hope is a confident expectation of what God has promised in His Word to come to pass and is based on your trust in Him and His faithfulness. The Bible says that

Abraham hoped against hope, which means he hoped in a promise from God that could only be performed by a miracle.

> **Romans 4:18a (KJV)**
> *18 Who against hope believed in hope…*

We can only hope for things we don't see. If we saw what we hoped for in the natural world, there would be no reason to hope for it. Therefore, hope is using your imagination to see something you desire to see manifest in the seen realm from the unseen realm. You hope for what you don't see with your imagination and then use your faith-filled words to manifest it.

> **Romans 8:24-25 (KJV)**
> *24 For we are saved by hope: but hope that is seen is not hope: for what a man seeth, why doth he yet hope for? 25 But if we hope for that we see not, then do we with patience wait for it.*

When using your faith to *"speak to a mountain,"* your belief has everything to do with your hope against hope. Only God can move the mountain through His power, and as we believe Him with our faith, we can speak to the mountain and make it move. However, you must fully understand where your hope comes in when speaking to a mountain and causing it to move successfully with your faith. Hope is just as important as faith when it comes to moving a mountain and seeing the impossible, which means your imagination is just as important as your faith when it comes to moving a mountain.

Your hope is the use of your imagination. When you are hoping for something, you are using your imagination. Hope through your imagination helps you see what you are believing for. So, if you attempt to speak to a mountain and make it move with your words but have not fully developed the inner image of it moving in the imagination of your heart, your words will be ineffective. Another way to say this is you could be wishing for something to happen with your words, but you have not fully developed the mental image of it in your heart, and therefore, it will not come to pass.

You will only experience with your words what you fully see with your imagination. For faith to work, hope must be developed in the imagination of the heart. Your heart has to see without any doubt what you are believing for. There cannot be any trace of doubt for your faith-filled words to work.

IMAGINATION WARFARE

Many believers do not spend enough time working on the imaginations of their hearts and fail to produce any results with their faith. You could have strongholds of fear, doubt, and unbelief in your heart, rendering your faith ineffective. Once all strongholds are dealt with and the Word of God perfects your imagination, your words will move mountains with your faith. This is called *Imagination Warfare*, and this is why the Bible teaches that we must cast down all wicked imaginations from the enemy.

> *2 Corinthians 10:3-6 (KJV)*
> *3 For though we walk in the flesh, we do not war after the flesh: 4 (For the weapons of our warfare are not carnal, but mighty through God to the pulling down of strong holds;)*

> *5 Casting down imaginations, and every high thing that exalteth itself against the knowledge of God, and bringing into captivity every thought to the obedience of Christ; 6 And having in a readiness to revenge all disobedience, when your obedience is fulfilled.*

This passage of Scripture helps us to understand the importance of taking every thought captive so it doesn't go into the heart and produce an evil imagination. The first line of defense is producing imaginations that line up with the Word of God through mind renewal. As you renew your mind to God's will, you are planting seeds in your heart that will produce a harvest in the Kingdom of God. It takes time to change your heart and line up your imagination to God's Word, and this is what Jesus revealed in the parable of the *Sower Sows the Word.* If you want a heart that produces imaginations from God, you must diligently focus your mind on God and His Word.

The enemy understands the power you have with your imagination and works at every possible level to fill you with images of fear, defeat, lack, poverty, death, sickness, hell, and destruction. If you do not battle those images in your heart, your faith will be ineffective, and you will experience whatever you imagine in your heart. If you only understand the power of words but don't fully deal with the source from which your words originate, you will not experience the victory you were promised in the Word of God. Faith works whenever there are no images of fear, doubt, and unbelief in the heart. If someone doesn't experience a promise being fulfilled, there must be vain images of fear, doubt, and unbelief in their heart because **GOD'S WORD IS TRUE.**

We see this truth in the story when the disciples could not cast a devil out of a child. They asked Jesus why they could not cast the devil out, and Jesus said it was because of their unbelief. This is the only story in the New Testament where a miracle didn't occur when someone was prayed for. Everyone who came to Jesus was healed 100% of the time because Jesus was using the power of His imagination with His faith-filled Words. The disciples failed to deliver the child with their words because of their unbelief.

> ### Matthew 17:14-20 (KJV)
>
> *14 And when they were come to the multitude, there came to him a certain man, kneeling down to him, and saying, 15 Lord, have mercy on my son: for he is lunatick, and sore vexed: for ofttimes he falleth into the fire, and oft into the water. 16 And I brought him to thy disciples, and they could not cure him. 17 **Then Jesus answered and said, O faithless and perverse generation, how long shall I be with you?** how long shall I suffer you? bring him hither to me. 18 And Jesus rebuked the devil; and he departed out of him: and the child was cured from that very hour. 19 **Then came the disciples to Jesus apart, and said, Why could not we cast him out? 20 And Jesus said unto them, Because of your unbelief:** for verily I say unto you, If ye have faith as a grain of mustard seed, ye shall say unto this mountain, Remove hence to yonder place; and it shall remove; and nothing shall be impossible unto you.*

When you talk to most Christians today about their imagination, they are clueless about what it is, how it works, or how they should use it according to the Word of God. But the Bible is very clear that we have an imagination, and it needs to be protected and utilized. When your understanding is opened to the power of your imagination, you will begin to see in the Scriptures how much God has to say about your imagination. The Bible will come alive in many ways you could ever imagine, and your faith will become more effective.

THE OBSERVER EFFECT

Science has made many breakthroughs in Quantum Physics that help us understand how the unseen world operates and functions. Quantum mechanics is the field of physics that explains how subatomic particles behave. Subatomic particles don't behave how we would generally expect them to behave. Understanding the Laws of Quantum Physics is highly valuable when understanding how your faith works. Quantum Physics has proven many truths found in the Word of God.

One of the laws scientists discovered in the Quantum World is the Observer Effect. The Observer Effect helps us understand the power of our imagination. The Observer Effect essentially revealed in the Quantum World that the observer can affect the behavior of subatomic particles by simply observing them. The unseen realm of subatomic particles or the base level of all of the elements that make up creation can be affected by observing it. The Observer Effect is simply observing a situation or phenomenon that changes it. It is changed by how you observe it with your imagination. Your imagination is connected to all of creation.

In Biblical terms, what you observe with your imagination affects the unseen *Realm of the Spirit.* What you see through your imagination will cause it to manifest in the seen world from the unseen world. If you use your imagination to see the promises of God found in the Word of God, you can affect the elements that the world is made of to line up with what you see in the imagination of your heart. This is why the Bible tells us to look not at things that are seen but unseen. The only way to observe and see the unseen realm is with your imagination, which is your inward eye.

> *2 Corinthians 4:18 (KJV)*
> *18 While we look not at the things which are seen, but at the things which are not seen: for the things which are seen are temporal; but the things which are not seen are eternal.*

Another way the Bible says this is for us to walk by faith and not by sight. Walking by faith is walking by seeing into the unseen realm with your hope through your imagination.

> *2 Corinthians 5:7 (KJV)*
> *7 (For we walk by faith, not by sight:)*

Another discovery in Quantum Physics is that every possible outcome of a quantum event already exists in a separate parallel dimension. They call this Superposition, which is another way of saying in Biblical terms that *it is already done.* Quantum Superposition is a fundamental principle in Quantum Mechanics that states a physical system can exist in multiple states simultaneously until it is measured or viewed. This helps you to understand when the Bible says we were healed – past tense (1 Peter 2:24). Since everything is already done and exists in the unseen world, all we have to do is observe this fact with our imagination and through our faith, we can cause it to manifest in the seen world. Superposition suggests that the observer (through their imagination) affects the possible outcome.

If you look at the world through an imagination filled with fear, you will experience what you fear, and this is why the Bible says over and over again not to fear. Fear comes with images from the unseen world, and these images will come to pass no matter what you say if the images of the heart are not dealt with. So, if you are going to see the promises of God come to pass through your words spoken in faith to move mountains, you must have a redeemed, pure, and fruitful imagination. Your imagination can only be redeemed when you fully understand God's perfect love for you. When your heart imagines God being there for you and helping you in your time of need, you will experience what you are hoping for. Perfect love casts out all fear because fear has torment.

> *1 John 4:18 (KJV)*
> *18 There is no fear in love; but perfect love casteth out fear: because fear hath torment. He that feareth is not made perfect in love.*

Now you can understand why God said nothing would be impossible for them in what they imagined to do at the Tower of Babel. Whatever you imagine in your heart will come to pass, not just what you say. God and the unseen world around you hear your words and the images found in your words. Mountains respond to words with an image of it moving, not just telling it to move. When you understand the mystery of your imagination and use it purposely, your world will change around you as you speak to it.

SELF-IMAGE

Another important aspect of your imagination is how you see yourself, which is your self-image. Your image from the standpoint of your imagination is what you think about who you are. To function as a mature son of God, you must see yourself in Christ and Christ in you. The only way to see yourself correctly in the *Realm of the Spirit* is to look to Jesus. However, you cannot look to Jesus, who you cannot see unless you use your imagination to see Him.

> *Hebrews 12:2 (KJV)*
> *2 Looking unto Jesus the author and finisher of our faith;*
> *who for the joy that was set before him endured the cross,*
> *despising the shame, and is set down at the right hand of the*
> *throne of God.*

When you use your imagination correctly to see who Jesus is, you are changed from glory to glory through the Word of God. As you change from glory to glory, you correctly see who you are in Christ in the imagination of your heart. Your *New Man* was made in the image of Christ.

> *2 Corinthians 3:18 (KJV)*
> *18 But we all, with open face beholding as in a glass the*
> *glory of the Lord, are changed into the same image from*
> *glory to glory, even as by the Spirit of the Lord.*

The enemy works hard to deceive people and blind them from discovering the truth of who they are in Christ. He blinds people's minds and prevents them from seeing the glorious Gospel message and coming into Christ's image. However, when the Gospel message is preached, it shines the glory of God on unbeliever's dark hearts and gives them hope of who they can be in Christ.

> ### 2 Corinthians 4:3-5 (KJV)
> *3 But if our gospel be hid, it is hid to them that are lost: 4* **In whom the god of this world hath blinded the minds of them which believe not, lest the light of the glorious gospel of Christ, who is the image of God, should shine unto them.** *5 For we preach not ourselves, but Christ Jesus the Lord; and ourselves your servants for Jesus' sake.*

A primary mission of Christ was to shine His light on humanity's evil heart and imagination so they could repent and choose to come into the image of who He is. The enemy and religious leaders hate this message and try to keep people from becoming like Christ in this world. Don't let anyone rob you of the truth of who you are in Christ. When you accepted Christ, you became a new creature made in Christ's exact image.

> ### 2 Corinthians 5:17 (KJV)
> *17* **Therefore if any man be in Christ, he is a new creature: old things are passed away; behold, all things are become new.**

MEDITATION

Meditation is a powerful way to establish in your renewed mind who you are in Christ. Meditation is where you use your mind and imagination to think about the truth of God's Word. The more you meditate on God's Word, the more it will change you. Seeing who you are in Christ through the power of your imagination will change you from the inside out. The more you look at Christ, the more you will become like Christ because you become what you look at. This is why God commands us to meditate on His Word day and night.

> **Joshua 1:8 (KJV)**
> *8 This book of the law shall not depart out of thy mouth; **but thou shalt meditate therein day and night,** that thou mayest observe to do according to all that is written therein: for then thou shalt make thy way prosperous, and then thou shalt have good success.*

When you use your imagination through meditation, you must visualize what you desire long enough to see it done inside yourself. You must focus intently on what you are looking at until you can see it clearly. You must also understand that God has already answered your prayer in the unseen realm. He is waiting for you to use your imagination to see what you are hoping for done and then manifest it with your prayer of faith.

Your imagination needs to stay focused on your desire until your desire is solidified within yourself and doesn't change through contrary images from the enemy. This means you have visualized an outcome using your imagination that won't leave you and doesn't change. Once you reach this level of focus, you will know you have the answer, and then it is time to speak to the mountain with your faith.

IMAGINATION GUIDELINES

1. Find somewhere quiet where you can meditate and visualize without being interrupted.

2. Turn off all devices that can cause a distraction, such as TV, laptops, mobile phones, etc.

3. Close your eyes and focus with the eyes of your heart on what you are desiring from God to manifest.

4. Meditate with your imagination until you can see yourself inheriting the promises of God.

5. Use your imagination to see yourself inheriting the promises of God from as many angles as possible.

6. Cast down any wicked imaginations contrary to what you are believing for and bring all of your thoughts captive to the obedience of Christ.

7. Practice 1-6 as many times in a day and for as many days as needed until you can see the promise of God within yourself.

8. Speak what you are imagining out loud and command it to come forth.

9. Enjoy inheriting the promises of God regularly.

We have also put together images of truth from the Word of God for you to meditate on. As you use your imagination on purpose, not letting the enemy use your imagination, you will start seeing your world change. The following list is only a guideline to help you get started by using your imagination. You can use your imagination to claim any promises in the Word of God.

IMAGINATION VISUALS

1. See what the Bible is saying rather than just reading it

2. See yourself the way the Bible describes you as a new creation in the Image of Christ

3. See what you can do in the Spirit

4. See yourself crucified with Christ and walking in the newness of life

5. See yourself loving God with all your heart, mind, soul, body, and strength

6. See yourself loving others as you love yourself and doing to them what you would want done to yourself

7. See yourself as a son of God

8. See and imagine yourself in Christ and Christ in you

9. See yourself as a new creation in Christ (A new species of being never created before)

10. See yourself hearing and obeying all the Words of Christ

11. See yourself anointed by God

12. See yourself as a Temple of the Holy Spirit

13. See yourself Anointed by the Holy Spirit

14. See yourself free in Christ

15. See yourself free from the dominion of sin

16. See yourself strong in the Lord and the power of His might

17. See yourself as an overcoming conqueror

18. See yourself winning every spiritual battle

19. See yourself defeating the enemy and putting your foot on his neck

20. See yourself as a master of the devil and his demons

21. See yourself speaking the Words of God – See your words as Spirit and Life

22. See yourself speaking words of Life to people

23. See yourself walking in the power of God

24. See yourself seated in Heavenly Places in Christ

25. See yourself inheriting all the promises of God

26. See yourself strong in the Lord and in the power of His might

27. See yourself in Christ having dominion over the enemy and all of his works

28. See yourself being able to do all things through Christ, who strengthens you

29. See yourself prosperous and in health even as your soul prospers

30. See the Holy Spirit filling your mind, soul, heart, and body

31. See the Holy Spirit filling every cell of your body

32. See the Holy Spirit healing any sick part of your body

33. See the Holy Spirit filling every part of your being

34. Imagine and see yourself doing "Greater Works" than Jesus did

35. See what you can do in the Spirit and operating in the anointing

36. See what you have in the Spirit – See yourself inheriting the Promises of God

37. See the specific promise you are looking to inherit

38. See God answering all of your prayers

39. See yourself blessed now and in the future

DAY OF PENTECOST

A hidden secret regarding your imagination can be found on the Day of Pentecost. On the Day of Pentecost in Acts Chapter 2, Jesus promised His disciples they would receive power when the Holy Spirit came on them. We know they spoke in other tongues when this event occurred, as the Holy Spirit gave them utterance. Those from other nations heard the early disciples speak the wonderful works of God in their own language. This experience directly ties back to the day when God changed mankind's language at the Tower of Babel. God, said that nothing would be restrained from them, which they have imagined to do. When God changed the people's language that day, they left the building of the tower of Babel and were scattered over the whole Earth.

The Day of Pentecost, in many ways, was not only a reversal of what happened at the Tower of Babel, but God imparted His imagination to the early believers who were baptized in the Holy Spirit. On this significant day, God restored His imagination into men's hearts and gave them a new language as a sign. Speaking in other tongues was a sign from God to bring to light man's heart again and remove vain imaginations from them. When your imaginations line up with God, you will speak the Word of God with boldness.

Not only can you use your imagination for God, but God desires to use your imagination to accomplish His purposes on the Earth. God is looking for those who will unite as ONE with Him and allow Him to accomplish His will on the Earth. When you acknowledge who you are in Christ and who He is in you, God can begin to accomplish what He sees in His imagination through your imagination. In essence, you have to allow your imagination to become one with God's imagination.

When you learn the power of your imagination, nothing will be restrained from what you desire to do. This chapter reveals the mysteries of the universe and how God created and controls the elements of the world. God uses His imagination, speaks, and creates what He sees within Himself. Once you learn the secret potential of your imagination and how it is interconnected with all matter, you are well on your way to making mountains move with your faith. Now is the time for the sons of

God to mature and use their imagination the way God intended for it to be used.

In conclusion, your imagination is more important and influential than you may have ever known. Your imagination plays an integral part in your daily and spiritual life. Nothing is impossible with your redeemed imagination. You will see mountains move as you discover this truth and use your imagination with your faith. Nothing will be restrained from all you imagine to do as you allow God to impart His imagination into your imagination.

YOUR IMAGINATION IS THE SECRET TO BRINGING INVISIBLE REALITIES TO THE VISIBLE WORLD!

CHAPTER 9

SPEAKING IN TONGUES

When God poured out His Spirit on the Day of Pentecost, the early Church was graced with one of the most spectacular and glorious gifts God could give humankind: the gift of the Holy Spirit, evidenced by speaking in other tongues. Speaking in other tongues is one of God's highest forms of spiritual awakening when you are baptized in the Holy Spirit. Early disciples of Christ baptized in the Holy Spirit received power from on high to work miracles as a promise from their Heavenly Father as they were given the ability to speak with a Heavenly language.

> *Luke 24:49 (KJV)*
> *49 And, behold, I send the promise of my Father upon you: but tarry ye in the city of Jerusalem, until ye be endued with power from on high.*

> *Acts 1:8 (KJV)*
> *8 But ye shall receive power, after that the Holy Ghost is come upon you: and ye shall be witnesses unto me both in*

Jerusalem, and in all Judaea, and in Samaria, and unto the uttermost part of the earth.

Speaking in tongues is like an old-fashioned mechanical generator that produces electricity by cranking the handle. The more the handle was cranked, the more electricity was produced. The more you speak in tongues, the more spiritual power you generate from the *Realm of the Spirit* in your soul and body. Once the power of God comes upon you, you can lay hands on the sick, and they will recover. Spiritual power is generated by allowing the Holy Spirit to speak through your voice in another language as you pray directly to God, enabling you to tap into **God's Divine Supernatural Miracle Working Power.**

On the Day of Pentecost, the initial evidence of being baptized in the Holy Spirit was speaking in other tongues. God used speaking in tongues as a sign to unbelievers while at the same time filling His disciples with miracle-working power. The Day of Pentecost was a reversal of what God did at the Tower of Babel, which we discussed in the previous chapter. The Day of Pentecost, recorded in Acts Chapter 2, was the first time in recorded history where God manifested Himself through the infilling of the Holy Spirit, evidenced by His followers speaking in other languages. This was a *special day* like no other!

> *Acts 2:1-11 (KJV)*
> *1 And when the day of Pentecost was fully come, they were all with one accord in one place. 2 And suddenly there came a sound from heaven as of a rushing mighty wind, and it filled all the house where they were sitting. 3 And there appeared unto them cloven tongues like as of fire, and it sat upon each of them. 4 **And they were all filled with the Holy***

*Ghost, and began to speak with other tongues, as the Spirit gave them utterance. 5 And there were dwelling at Jerusalem Jews, devout men, out of every nation under heaven. 6 Now when this was noised abroad, the multitude came together, and were confounded, because that every man heard them speak in his own language. 7 And they were all amazed and marvelled, saying one to another, Behold, are not all these which speak Galilaeans? 8 **And how hear we every man in our own tongue, wherein we were born?** 9 Parthians, and Medes, and Elamites, and the dwellers in Mesopotamia, and in Judaea, and Cappadocia, in Pontus, and Asia, 10 Phrygia, and Pamphylia, in Egypt, and in the parts of Libya about Cyrene, and strangers of Rome, Jews and proselytes, 11 Cretes and Arabians, **we do hear them speak in our tongues the wonderful works of God.***

As the early Church grew and matured, God called a man named Saul through a Divine encounter and renamed him Paul. Paul became known as the Apostle Paul and went on to write most of the New Testament. God chose the Apostle Paul to understand the more profound revelations concerning the Gospel and the finished work of Christ. One of the most important revelations he received was a deep understanding of the power of speaking in tongues. None of the other Apostles wrote anything near what the Apostle Paul taught concerning speaking in tongues in the New Testament.

Many of the truths Paul taught about speaking in tongues have been lost today in the modern Church. Some Churches even teach against speaking in tongues. The Apostle Paul taught not to forbid believers from speaking in tongues. 1 Corinthians 14:39 (KJV): *"Wherefore, brethren, covet to prophesy, and forbid not to speak with tongues."*

Every author that the Holy Spirit used to write the New Testament spoke in tongues, and God assumed that everyone who accepted Christ as their Lord would be baptized in the Holy Spirit and speak in a Heavenly language at some point in their lives. Throughout history, you can trace speaking in tongues to almost every significant move of God, where miracles have been involved since the time of Christ. Speaking in Tongues has and always will play an essential role in the New Testament Church until the day Christ returns.

For your *Eyes to Be Open* to the *Realm of The Spirit,* you must understand the impact and influence speaking in tongues has on your spiritual life. When you comprehend the scope and value of speaking in tongues, you will prioritize it daily. Speaking in tongues aligns and empowers your soul with your newly created spirit. God has hidden many mysteries in the speaking of tongues that you need to know to advance in the Kingdom of God. Frequent and daily speaking in tongues will propel you into the *Realms of the Spirit* where you transcend into the limitless possibilities of God.

There is a difference between the initial evidence of speaking in tongues when you are baptized in the Spirit, the gift of tongues as part of the nine gifts of the Spirit with interpretation, and your personal prayer language. We are teaching about your personal Heavenly prayer language, which is meant to be private between you and God. The gift of tongues with interpretation is a different manifestation as one of the nine gifts of the Holy Spirit that edifies the Church. When you are baptized in the Holy

Spirit, you will speak in other tongues as evidence that the power of the Spirit of God came upon you.

It cannot be underestimated the importance of speaking in tongues in your prayer life when it comes to growing in Christ and *Opening Your Eyes*. The Apostle Paul said that he spoke in tongues more than the whole Corinthian Church. Paul spent as much time as he could speaking in other tongues. The only reason someone would speak in their Heavenly language to this degree is because they would have to understand how critical it was to their spiritual life and all of the benefits that came with it. When you embrace the power and necessity of speaking in tongues, you will speak in other tongues as much as you can daily.

> ### *1 Corinthians 14:18 (KJV)*
> *18 I thank my God, I speak with tongues more than ye all:*

Some believers will have the initial evidence of speaking in tongues when they are baptized in the Holy Spirit but may not have the gift of tongues to edify the Church. However, everyone who is baptized in the Holy Spirit is given the ability to pray directly to God in their own Heavenly language, which they can pray at will with the help of the Holy Spirit. Once you perceive the importance of speaking in tongues, you will desire to speak in other tongues daily as much as possible.

Speaking in tongues is generated from your spirit and not your mind. You bypass your mind while you are speaking in tongues. Because you bypass your mind, you can speak in tongues while doing other tasks, thus giving you the ability to pray without ceasing (1 Thessalonians 5:17). Your initial experience of speaking in tongues when you were baptized into the Holy Spirit was only an initiation into the *Realm of the Spirit.*

From that point forward, speaking in other tongues should be a continual experience for the rest of your life. Living streams of water flow out of your belly and through your mouth as you speak in other tongues and should never dry up! At first, speaking in tongues takes discipline, which turns into a habit, and then the habit of speaking in other tongues becomes an addiction the more you exercise this gift.

The Holy Spirit will not help you unless you pray and ask for His help. Therefore, praying in the Spirit is not an option for Christians but a mandate. God can do nothing for humanity unless someone asks for His help. Speaking in other tongues is one of the most potent and effective ways to pray because you are allowing the Holy Spirit to pray the perfect will of God through you. Your victory against enemies and difficult situations depends upon the effectiveness and frequency of your prayers. Therefore, spend as much time praying in the Spirit by speaking in other tongues until you get a breakthrough.

> **Romans 8:26-27 (KJV)**
> *26 Likewise the Spirit also helpeth our infirmities: for we know not what we should pray for as we ought: but the Spirit itself maketh intercession for us with groanings which cannot be uttered. 27 And he that searcheth the hearts knoweth what is the mind of the Spirit, because he maketh intercession for the saints according to the will of God.*

Your newly created spirit was never made to remain silent within you. The *New Man* is expressed and given a voice as you speak in your Heavenly language. When you speak in other tongues, you allow your *New Man* to speak directly to God through His Spirit. Your mouth was intended to be a spout where the glory comes out, not a dam that stops the *Rivers of Living Waters* from flowing. Speaking in tongues is one of the highest forms of communication between you and God. *Speaking in Other Tongues is a Doorway into the Supernatural Realm of the Spirit that Causes Many Spectacular Miraculous Events to Occur.*

We have listed below many profound benefits and rewards of speaking in tongues to help you understand the importance of your Heavenly language. To spiritually mature and *Open Your Spiritual Eyes*, you must exercise and grow in this gift. There are many profound revelations to speaking in tongues, so you should speak in other tongues frequently throughout the day. Glorious experiences, Divine revelations, and empowerment await you as you speak in other tongues. The more you speak in tongues, the more you will grow, be filled with power, walk in the strength of God, enter God's rest, be refreshed, and *Your Spiritual Eyes* become more open to the *Realm of the Spirit.*

BENEFITS OF SPEAKING IN TONGUES

1. Activates the miraculous power of God. Speaking in other tongues generates the power of God within you and on you. The more you speak in tongues, the more power you store up (Acts 1:8; Acts 4:29-32; Mark 16:15-20; Luke 24:49)

2. Imparts boldness to speak the Word of God and removes fear (Acts 4:29-31; Romans 8:15; 2 Timothy 1:7)

3. Strengthens your inner man with might and joy – Makes you strong in the Lord and in the power of His might (Ephesians 3:16; Ephesians 6:10; Colossians 1:10-11)

4.   Personal transformation – Helps you mature in Christ – Reminds you of the Words of Christ (John 16:12-15; Ephesians 4:4-16)

5.   Gives you power over sin and the works of the flesh (Romans 8:13; Galatians 5:16-21)

6.   Draws wisdom from your spirit into your mind (1 Corinthians 2:7)

7.   You speak mysteries to God (1 Corinthians 14:2)

8.   Downloads revelations from God (1 Corinthians 2:9-16)

9.   The Holy Spirit intercedes the perfect will of God through you, causing all things to work together for your good (Romans 8:26-28)

10. Keeps you in the peace of God in your heart and mind that surpasses all understanding (John 20:21-22; Philippians 4:6-7)

11. Builds you and the Church up through edification as the Temple of the Holy Spirit for God to inhabit (1 Corinthians 14:4; Ephesians 2:18-22)

12. Helps you to be continually led by the Holy Spirit (Romans 8:14)

13. Builds up your most holy faith (Jude 1:20)

14. Keeps you in the love of God – Facilitates your intimacy with God (Jude 1:21)

15. Puts & keeps the whole armor of God on you
    (Ephesians 6:10-20)

16. Fills you with the Holy Spirit (Ephesians 5:18)

17. Fights against your enemies (warfare) – Praying in warfare
    tongues is a weapon that destroys the works of the enemy
    (Ephesians 6:10-20)

18. God communicates images into your imagination from His
    imagination – God builds your prophetic future through your
    imagination as you speak in tongues
    (Genisis 11:1-9; Acts 2:1-12)

19. Enters you into the rest of God
    (Isaiah 28:11-12)

20. Refreshes your soul – Speaking in other tongues is how you
    drink of the *Water of Life* flowing out of your belly
    (Isaiah 28:11-12; John 4:5-15; John 7:37-39)

21. Helps you pray when you don't know what to pray
    (Romans 8:26)

22. Praying in tongues *"without ceasing"* tames your tongue and
    makes your words more effective (Isaiah 59:21;
    1 Thessalonians 5:17; James 3:1-18)

23. Activates and stirs up (rekindles & revives the fire) the nine
    gifts of the Holy Spirit inside you
    (1 Corinthians 12:1-11; 2 Timothy 1:6-7)

24. Helps you walk in the nine fruits of the Holy Spirit (Galatians 5:22-25)

25. Allows you to come boldly to the Throne of grace and obtain mercy – A Secret Place of communication between you and God (Psalm 91:1; Matthew 6:6-8; Hebrews 4:16)

ENTERING HIS REST

Speaking in tongues fulfills a prophecy from the Old Testament Book of Isaiah, written over 700 years before the Book of Acts. God revealed to the Prophet Isaiah that He would speak to people through stammering lips and another tongue, but unfortunately, it says they will not hear Him when He speaks to them in this way.

> *Isaiah 28:10-13 (KJV)*
>
> *10 For precept must be upon precept, precept upon precept; line upon line, line upon line; here a little, and there a little:* ***11 For with stammering lips and another tongue will he speak to this people. 12 To whom he said, This is the rest wherewith ye may cause the weary to rest; and this is the refreshing: yet they would not hear.*** *13 But the word of the Lord was unto them precept upon precept, precept upon precept; line upon line, line upon line; here a little, and there a little; that they might go, and fall backward, and be broken, and snared, and taken.*

In this prophetic Scripture, God revealed through stammering lips that the weary would find rest, which would be the refreshing. When you tie this prophetic word with the revelation found in Hebrews 4 about entering into God's *Rest*, your faith takes on a whole new meaning. Speaking in tongues helps you enter into the *Promised Rest* of the *Gospel* as you speak in tongues by faith. Speaking in tongues is a secret to inheriting God's promises and entering His *Rest*.

> ### *Hebrews 4:1-11 (KJV)*
>
> *1 **Let us therefore fear, lest, a promise being left us of entering into his rest, any of you should seem to come short of it.** 2 For unto us was the gospel preached, as well as unto them: but the word preached did not profit them, not being mixed with faith in them that heard it. 3 **For we which have believed do enter into rest, as he said, As I have sworn in my wrath, if they shall enter into my rest:** although the works were finished from the foundation of the world. 4 For he spake in a certain place of the seventh day on this wise, And God did rest the seventh day from all his works. 5 And in this place again, **If they shall enter into my rest. 6 Seeing therefore it remaineth that some must enter therein, and they to whom it was first preached entered not in because of unbelief:** 7 Again, he limiteth a certain day, saying in David, To day, after so long a time; as it is said, To day if ye will hear his voice, harden not your hearts. 8 For if Jesus had given them rest, then would he not afterward have spoken of another day. 9 **There remaineth therefore a rest to the people of God. 10 For he that is entered into his rest, he also hath ceased from his own works, as God did from his. 11 Let us labour therefore to enter into that rest, lest any man fall after the same example of unbelief.***

If we are to enter the *Rest* of God, we need to labor in speaking in tongues until we inherit all that God paid for in Christ. The Father gave us the Holy Spirit in His Divine wisdom, but we are responsible for speaking in tongues to enter the *Rest* of God. As you speak in tongues, you are laboring in the Spirit, not to get God to do something, but for you to inherit what He already accomplished in the death, burial, and resurrection of Jesus. Speaking in tongues enables you to enter your Promised Land, which can only be found in the Gospel. The Promised Land represents living a life in which you inherit all the promises of God.

When you speak in tongues, your *Eyes Are Opened,* and you are built up, awakened, and empowered by the Holy Spirit. As you speak in tongues, the Holy Spirit gives you the strength, wisdom, power, and ability to *Open Your Eyes to* manifest who you were called to be and inherit all that God has for you. The Holy Spirit will make you a power to be reckoned with when you speak in tongues regularly. The enemies of God that are possessing your Promised Land are no match for a faith-filled, on-fire, tongue-talking child of God. God will give you the life of your *"Spiritual Dreams"* as you learn the necessity, importance, and power of speaking in tongues.

As we bring this chapter to a close, you can see that speaking in tongues will change the spiritual landscape of your life like few things can. Speaking in tongues plays a significant role in your *Eyes Being Opened.* Once you learn the value of speaking in tongues, your prayer life will be filled with the power and presence of God. You will move into new dimensions of the glory of God and *Realms of the Spirit* by frequently speaking in tongues. Speaking in tongues is the key that unlocks the treasure chest of all that Jesus paid for. The power of God transforms every believer who discovers the secret of speaking in tongues. Now is the time to answer the call of speaking in tongues, release the power of God, enter His *Rest*, and inherit your Promised Land!

THE AMOUNT OF TIME YOU PUT FORTH IN PRAYER TO ADMINISTER THE HOLY SPIRIT THROUGH SPEAKING IN TONGUES IS THE MEASURE HE WILL WORK THROUGH YOU AND FOR YOU!

CHAPTER 10

PREACHING & TEACHING

One vital factor in opening believer's spiritual eyes is the role anointed preaching and teaching play in their lives. God has ordained that by preaching and teaching His Word through the gift of five-fold ministers, people would be saved and taught the profound mysteries of His Kingdom. Without anointed preaching and teaching, many unbelievers and believers would remain spiritually blind and in the dark regarding God's Word and the *Realm of the Spirit.*

The hidden mysteries of the Kingdom of God and the Gospel are not just to be read and understood only by His written Word. Anointed ministers are sent by God to proclaim His hidden truths and message of salvation. God ordains His anointed ministers to preach and teach the mysteries of the Kingdom of God found in the Word of God. God first opens the spiritual eyes of the minister and then uses them to *Open the Eyes* of those they are sent to. We can see this truth revealed in the life of Paul the Apostle when he encountered Christ on the way to Damascus and was commissioned to *Open the Eyes* of the Gentiles, turn them from darkness to light, and from the power of satan unto God by Jesus.

Acts 26:16-18 (KJV)

*16 But rise, and stand upon thy feet: for I have appeared unto thee for this purpose, to make thee a minister and a witness both of these things which thou hast seen, and of those things in the which I will appear unto thee; 17 Delivering thee from the people, and from the Gentiles, unto whom now I send thee, 18 **To open their eyes, and to turn them from darkness to light,** and from the power of Satan unto God, that they may receive forgiveness of sins, and inheritance among them which are sanctified by faith that is in me.*

Paul opened the eyes of the Gentiles to the revelations God gave him, which were revealed in his teaching, preaching, and letters to the early Churches. Since the New Testament was established, every believer who has read the Bible has benefited from the letters Paul wrote. He was given insight into mysteries that not even many of the Apostles of the Lord received concerning the destiny of the Church, New Man, Holy Spirit, Return of Christ, End Days, Kingdom of God, Gifts of the Spirit, Bride of Christ, Spiritual Warfare, and many more spiritual truths. Many of the revelations in this book come from the Apostle Paul's profound teachings in the letters he wrote to the Churches he was called to. The Apostle Peter even said that some of the things that Paul wrote about are hard to understand, and they that are unlearned wrest (distort) as they do other Scriptures.

2 Peter 3:15-16 (KJV)

*15 And account that the longsuffering of our Lord is salvation; **even as our beloved brother Paul also according*** *to the wisdom given unto him hath written unto you; 16 As also in all his epistles, speaking in them of these things; in which are some things hard to be understood, which they that are unlearned and unstable wrest, as they do also the other scriptures,* unto their own destruction.

God ordained that by sending anointed ministers who would preach and teach the Word of God, humanity would be saved. For some, this would seem foolish, but through the wisdom of God, it pleased Him that people would be saved if they believed what was preached.

1 Corinthians 1:21 (KJV)

21 For after that in the wisdom of God the world by wisdom knew not God, **it pleased God by the foolishness of preaching to save them that believe.**

The Apostle Peter declared that the angels desire to look into what is preached in the Gospel through the Holy Spirit sent down from Heaven. Angels desire to see all that God worked on behalf of humanity through the finished work of Christ and all the blessings that come with His redemptive plan.

1 Peter 1:12 (KJV)

12 Unto whom it was revealed, that not unto themselves, but unto us they did minister the things, **which are now reported unto you by them that have preached the gospel unto you with the Holy Ghost sent down from heaven; which things the angels desire to look into.**

Jesus Himself chose to come as a humble preacher to reveal the plan and Word of God. Jesus preached the truth of the Gospel to large crowds who came to see the miracles He was performing while teaching them the mysteries of the Kingdom of God. Jesus was the first faith preacher.

> *Matthew 4:23 (KJV)*
> *23 **And Jesus went about all Galilee, teaching in their synagogues, and preaching the gospel of the kingdom,** and healing all manner of sickness and all manner of disease among the people.*

After Jesus rose from the dead, He commanded His disciples to go into the world and teach all nations to observe everything whatsoever He commanded them while He was on the Earth. This is called the *Great Commission!* God has revealed that through preaching and teaching of the Gospel, the eyes of the spiritually blind would be open. After you accept Jesus, it is critically important for you to continue listening to anointed ministers to grow in your walk with God and *Open Your Eyes.*

> *Matthew 28:18-20 (KJV)*
> *18 And Jesus came and spake unto them, saying, All power is given unto me in heaven and in earth. 19 **Go ye therefore, and teach all nations,** baptizing them in the name of the Father, and of the Son, and of the Holy Ghost: 20 **Teaching them to observe all things whatsoever I have commanded you:** and, lo, I am with you always, even unto the end of the world. Amen*

The Apostle Paul wrote in the Book of Romans that people wouldn't know how to call on the Lord and what to believe if a preacher was not sent to them. He said faith would be the product of hearing a preacher sent by God who preached the good tidings of the Gospel of Peace. He taught that faith came by hearing the Word of God being preached by a sent preacher and not just reading the Bible.

> ### Romans 10:13-17 (KJV)
> *13 For whosoever shall call upon the name of the Lord shall be saved. 14 **How then shall they call on him in whom they have not believed? and how shall they believe in him of whom they have not heard? and how shall they hear without a preacher?** 15 And how shall they preach, except they be sent? as it is written, How beautiful are the feet of them that preach the gospel of peace, and bring glad tidings of good things! 16 But they have not all obeyed the gospel. For Esaias saith, Lord, who hath believed our report? 17 **So then faith cometh by hearing, and hearing by the word of God.***

This passage reveals the importance and value of hearing anointed preachers and teachers because it produces faith in your heart if you believe. Many powerful ministers throughout history have opened the eyes of millions through preaching, teaching, and writing books. Men and women of God have been used to change nations and alter the destiny of humankind through the preaching of the Gospel. The early disciples were able to change the pagan nation of Rome into a Christian nation through the preaching and teaching of the Gospel. The early believers also converted many nations to Christianity, and the world became a better place as the Gospel of Christ advanced through *Opening the Eyes* of those sitting in darkness. Untold millions of people have been spiritually awakened and saved because of the work and sacrifice of ministers God sent.

For your eyes to be spiritually open and grow up in Christ, you must sit under, listen to, and adhere to as much anointed teaching and preaching as possible. We recommend opening yourself to established men of God in as many camps as possible. What we mean by camps is that there are diverse Divine messages, and some anointed ministers have more understanding and revelation in certain subjects of the Word of God than other ministers. Some Christian camps specialize in healing, faith, grace, anointing, gifts of the Spirit, prophecy, mind renewal, new man, deliverance, speaking in tongues, power of God, holiness, and more. The more you receive from ministers specializing in a subject, the more you will grow.

Since the invention of the internet, we now have access to some of the best-anointed ministries God has sent to the Earth at our fingertips. Yes, you have to be careful not to listen and receive from false teachers, but if you can find powerful preachers and teachers through the leading of the Lord, you will grow more spiritually than you ever could on your own. You can only grow so far in your study of the Word, but with the help of anointed ministers, your *Eyes Will Be Opened* as they reveal what God has shown them.

Once you discover a powerful anointed ministry, we recommend listening to them as much as possible throughout your day. You can also listen to a message over and over if you spiritually need it and it is ministering to you. For your *Eyes to Be Open*, we recommend listening to as much preaching and teaching as possible. Going to Church once a week to hear a nice little sermon will never be enough for you to mature and spiritually *Open Your Eyes*. As great as your pastor may be, he should also be recommending other ministries for you to receive from. You need an impartation from all five-fold ministries to mature in Christ!

> ***Ephesians 4:11-15 (KJV)***
> ***11 And he gave some, apostles; and some, prophets; and some, evangelists; and some, pastors and teachers; 12 For the perfecting of the saints, for the work of the ministry, for the edifying of the body of Christ: 13 Till we all come in the unity of the faith, and of the knowledge of the Son of God, unto a perfect man, unto the measure of the stature of the fulness of Christ:*** *14 That we henceforth be no more children, tossed to and fro, and carried about with every wind of doctrine, by the sleight of men, and cunning craftiness, whereby they lie in wait to deceive; 15 But speaking the truth in love,* ***may grow up into him in all things, which is the head, even Christ:***

While you listen to anointed preaching and teaching, you receive revelational impartations into your soul that help you advance in the *Realms of the Spirit*. God did not call us to walk this Christian life alone; you need to be discipled by others for your spiritual eyes to be opened. Discipleship is best when one and one, like in the case of Elisha with Elijah, but you can also be discipled in powerful ways by listening to anointed messages regularly. Many great Bible Schools can also teach the foundation of God's Word, and help you *Open Your Spiritual Eyes.*

Because receiving from anointed preaching of the Word is so powerful, the enemy will work hard to stop people from hearing, understanding, and doing what is preached. The enemy knows anyone who receives the

Word of God and understands it will break free from his control and oppression. This is why the first person mentioned in the parable of the *Sower Sows the Word* has the Word stolen from him by the devil through lack of understanding.

> ### Matthew 13:18-19 (KJV)
> *18 Hear ye therefore the parable of the sower. 19* ***When any one heareth the word of the kingdom, and understandeth it not, then cometh the wicked one, and catcheth away that which was sown in his heart.*** *This is he which received seed by the way side.*

The Bible also says that the god of this world has blinded the minds of them, which believe not lest the light of the glorious Gospel of Christ, who is the image of God, should shine on them. A lot of spiritual warfare occurs when the Gospel is taught and preached. But, if you commit to intently listening while adhering to what is being proclaimed, you will break into new *Realms of the Spirit.*

> ### 2 Corinthians 4:3-5 (KJV)
> *3 But if our gospel be hid, it is hid to them that are lost: 4* ***In whom the god of this world hath blinded the minds of them which believe not, lest the light of the glorious gospel of Christ, who is the image of God, should shine unto them.*** *5* ***For we preach not ourselves, but Christ Jesus the Lord;*** *and ourselves your servants for Jesus' sake.*

The Apostle Paul admonished Timothy to preach the Word and be instant in and out of season because the time would come when people would not endure sound doctrine. He also said that some would turn away people's ears from the truth and be turned to fables.

> *2 Timothy 4:2-4 (KJV)*
> *2 **Preach the word; be instant in season, out of season**; reprove, rebuke, exhort with all long suffering and doctrine. 3 For the time will come when they will not endure sound doctrine; but after their own lusts shall they heap to themselves teachers, having itching ears; 4 **And they shall turn away their ears from the truth, and shall be turned unto fables.***

Paul taught his disciple Timothy to take heed to himself and the doctrine and to continue in them and that by doing this, he would save himself and those who heard him. This shows the importance of hearing anointed preaching and teaching. Your eternal salvation depends on what you hear being preached.

> *1 Timothy 4:16 (KJV)*
> *16 **Take heed unto thyself, and unto the doctrine; continue in them: for in doing this thou shalt both save thyself, and them that hear thee.***

Opening someone's eyes takes spiritual warfare. A powerful man of God will speak God's Word with authority, power and strength, and when they proclaim the Word of God, captives are set free, and people's eyes are opened to the truth of the Gospel. God calls His anointed ministers to take His Word and wield it as a sword to tear down strongholds, vain imaginations, false doctrines, and lies of the enemy. Through the bold preaching of the Word, God's sword of the Spirit will turn people to God as their eyes are opened from the darkness and spiritual lies that have bound them.

> *Hebrews 4:12 (KJV)*
> *12 **For the word of God is quick, and powerful, and sharper than any twoedged sword,** piercing even to the dividing asunder of soul and spirit, and of the joints and marrow, and is a discerner of the thoughts and intents of the heart.*

BEREANS

A minister sent by God always has many Scriptures to back their teaching and preaching. Backing what you preach with Scriptures is especially important regarding new revelations or revelations the body of Christ has not heard in their generation. When Paul, the Apostle, was preaching and teaching, he revealed hidden mysteries that had never been revealed on the Earth but could still be found in the Old Testament. God gave the Apostle Paul insight into the glorious inheritance given to the New Testament Church by all Christ accomplished at the Cross. Once God revealed these hidden truths to Paul, he was able to enlighten the New Testament Church.

> *Galatians 1:11-12 (KJV)*
> *11 **But I certify you, brethren, that the gospel which was preached of me is not after man. 12 For I neither received it of man, neither was I taught it, but by the revelation of Jesus Christ.***

When Apostle Paul traveled to the many cities he was sent to, he was attacked and challenged for the new teachings he proclaimed about Christ by the Romans, and also the Jews who were dispersed abroad. Berea is one of the cities Paul entered that accepted him after being attacked in the ancient city of Thessalonica. In the city of Berea, Paul found a group of noble Jews who he preached the mysteries of Christ in their synagogue. This group of Jews had the best approach to the new truths they heard from the Apostle Paul. The Bible says they received the Word with all readiness of mind and searched the Scriptures daily to see if what Paul was preaching was true.

> *Acts 17:10-12 (KJV)*
> *10 And the brethren immediately sent away Paul and Silas by night unto* **Berea***: who coming thither went into the synagogue of the Jews. 11* **These were more noble than those in Thessalonica, in that they received the word with all readiness of mind, and searched the scriptures daily, whether those things were so.** *12 Therefore many of them believed; also of honourable women which were Greeks, and of men, not a few.*

The Bereans responded to the preaching of Paul in a receptive way while studying the Scriptures themselves, which is how every believer should react when they hear an anointed message. As powerful as a minister sent from God can be, it is also the responsibility of those hearing what is taught and preached to search out for themselves the truth being presented to them. God never intended His people to blindly follow any minister without doing their own due diligence. A genuine minister of the Gospel will always lead those who listen to them back to the authority of the Scriptures and stir a deep hunger within them to study the Word of God for themselves.

As the minister of God *Opens Your Eyes*, you *Open Your Own Eyes* when you joyfully and earnestly take what is preached and study it for yourself. A minister can only take you so far, and then it is up to the hearer to take responsibility and study God's Word independently in their personal time with the Lord. You will spiritually mature and *Open Your Eyes* when you combine anointed teaching and preaching with personal research in the Word of God. God has always intended for His ministers and people to have the same access and accountability to His Word.

After Jesus rose from the dead, it says He opened the understanding of His disciples so they might understand the Scriptures. Jesus revealed hidden truths in the writings of Moses, the Prophets, and the Psalms. The Apostles had read these verses for many years without understanding they were prophesying about Christ's sufferings and rising from the dead on the third day. These Scriptures were hidden in plain sight! The Apostles could now study hidden truths in the Word of God because Jesus *Opened their Eyes*.

> ### Luke 24:44-47 (KJV)
> *44 And he said unto them, These are the words which I spake unto you, while I was yet with you, that all things must be fulfilled, **which were written in the law of Moses, and in the prophets, and in the psalms, concerning me.** 45 **Then opened he their understanding, that they might understand the scriptures,** 46 And said unto them, **Thus it is written,** and thus it behooved Christ to suffer, and to rise from the dead the third day: 47 And that repentance and*

remission of sins should be preached in his name among all nations, beginning at Jerusalem.

In conclusion, we cannot emphasize enough the importance of hearing anointed preaching and teaching. As Christians, we should listen and feast on the Word proclaimed by God's anointed ministers as much as possible. You will enter new *Realms of the Spirit* by tapping into the revelations God has given His five-fold leaders. For your eyes to be open, it is up to you to ask God to lead you to the messages you need to hear for your spiritual growth and then research what you hear in the Word of God on your own. When you listen, research, and do what is being preached and taught, you will manifest God more in your life, *Open Your Eyes,* mature spiritually, receive breakthroughs, and inherit the promises of God.

PEOPLE WILL TRAVEL ACROSS THE WORLD TO HEAR THE WISDOM OF GOD BEING PREACHED BY AN ANOINTED MAN OF GOD!

CHAPTER 11

ACKNOWLEDGEMENTS

It is imperative as a Christian to acknowledge all Christ accomplished and made us to be in Him when He died, was buried, rose again, and sat down on the Father's right hand. Your mind is renewed once you reach a greater spiritual understanding of what Christ has done for you and walk in all His blessings. By acknowledging what Christ has done, the eyes of your understanding become open to what He placed inside you, and your faith becomes more effective. In this chapter, we will help you learn how to acknowledge all that has already happened inside you when you accepted Jesus as your Lord.

Philemon 1:6 (KJV)
*6 That the communication of thy faith may become effectual by the **acknowledging** of every good thing which is in you in Christ Jesus.*

Acknowledging means accepting, agreeing with, and recognizing the existence of a truth, perceiving, and verbally confessing. As you believe you received through *acknowledging* what God has done for you and placed in you, you experience more of it in your life. God's Divine life and power are experienced in the believer's life as their knowledge of Him increases from the Word of God. The more you know and acknowledge what Christ has placed in you, the more spiritual blessings you will experience. Everything you have been given and will receive from God has already been given to you, but you must perceive and acknowledge what God gave you so you can experience it in your life. Acknowledging is a powerful way to manifest spiritual blessings that exist in the unseen realm.

> *2 Peter 1:2-3 (KJV)*
> *2 Grace and peace be multiplied unto you **through the knowledge of God,** and of Jesus our Lord, 3 According as his divine power hath given unto us all things that pertain unto life and godliness, **through the knowledge of him** that hath called us to glory and virtue:*

When you became born-again, God made you a son of God by the Holy Spirit. It is up to us to research the Scriptures to learn what was placed in us, and it is also up to us to acknowledge who we are in Christ. A powerful way to acknowledge what Christ placed in you is to confess the truth of God's Word daily. The more you acknowledge and confess the Word of God over your life, the more you will be transformed into the image of God's dear Son. As you perceive with your spiritual eyes, believe, acknowledge, and confess with your mouth daily what is in your spirit, it will manifest more in your life and renew your mind. As your mind is renewed, you will think more like Christ and become and have what He says you have.

Below is a weekly list to help you acknowledge all God has done for you. You can also look up each Scripture to see the truth of what Christ has done for you, placed inside of you, and made you to be. For these acknowledgments to work and impact your life to where your mind is transformed and you believe them, you must read, meditate on, acknowledge, and confess them daily as many times as possible. Over time, you will start to see changes in your thinking, which will also affect your heart. These are necessary changes for you to see your life transformed by the Gospel. These acknowledgments are broken into daily confessions that, over time and repetition, will have a powerful impact on your life. These acknowledgments are also written in the first person, assuming you are living God's Word. There is great power in remembering through acknowledgments of all God has done for us.

These *Daily Acknowledgements* can and should be spoken one to three times a day or more. You can say these acknowledgments in the morning, at lunch, and before you go to bed. The more you verbally acknowledge what is in you, the more you will see changes in your mind and heart. Remember, you are responsible for your spiritual growth.

MONDAY ACKNOWLEDGEMENTS

1. I am loved by the Father as much as He loves His Son. (John 17:23)

2. The love that God has for Jesus is in me. (John 17:26)

3. The Father loves me so much that He gave His only begotten Son to die for me so that I could be saved and have Everlasting Life. (John 3:16)

4. The Father sent His Son not to condemn me, but that through Him I would be saved. (John 3:17)

5. The Father loves me because I love Jesus and know that Jesus came out from God. (John 16:27)

6. The love of God is shed abroad in my heart by the Holy Spirit that was given to me. (Romans 5:5)

7. God showed His love for me when He had Christ die for me, even when I was a sinner. (Romans 5:8)

8. Jesus had the greatest love in that He laid down His life for me. (John 15:3)

9. God has great love for me, even when I was dead in sins; He quickened me with Christ and raised me up, and made me sit together in Heavenly places in Christ Jesus. (Ephesians 2:4-6)

10. My Father in Heaven loves me more than my earthly father and that is why He chastens me. (Hebrews 12:5-11)

11. The Father bestowed His love upon me so that I could be called a son of God. (1 John 3:1)

12. The Father and the Son manifest themselves to me and make their abode with me because I love God by having and keeping His commandments. (John 14:21-23)

13. I love God because He first loved me. (1 John 4:19)

14. I keep myself in the love of God and look for the mercy of my Lord Jesus Christ unto Eternal Life. (Jude 1:21)

15. Nothing can separate me from God's love, which is in Christ Jesus my Lord. (Romans 8:38-39)

16. I love God with all my heart, mind, soul, and strength. (Mark 12:30)

17. I love my neighbor as myself. (Matthew 22:39)

18. I do unto others as I would want done unto me. (Matthew 7:12)

19. I walk in the perfect love of God and cast out fear. (1 John 4:18)

20. God loves me with an Everlasting Love. (Jeremiah 31:3)

21. All things work together for my good because I love God, and I'm called according to His purpose. (Romans 8:28)

22. My eyes see, my ears hear, and my heart understands the things God has prepared for me because I love Him. (1 Corinthians 2:9)

23. I am in the Family of Jesus because I do the will of God. (Mark 3:31-35)

24. I am saved because I believe that God raised Jesus from the dead and I confess Him as my Lord. (Romans 10:8-10)

25. Jesus is my Lord because I do the things which He says. (Luke 6:46)

26. I love the Lord because He heard my voice and my supplications. (Psalm 116:1)

27. I will call upon the Lord as long as I live because He has inclined His ear unto me. (Psalm 116:2)

28. I am blessed because I hear and keep the Word of God. (Luke 11:27-28)

29. I have been blessed with all spiritual blessings in Heavenly places in Christ. (Ephesians 1:3)

30. God dwells in me and walks in me because I am a Temple of the Living God. (2 Corinthians 6:16)

31. God receives me because I came out from the world, separated myself and I don't touch the unclean thing. (2 Corinthians 6:17)

32. I have a new heart and a new spirit. (Ezekiel 36:25-37)

33. My love is made perfect, and I will have boldness in the Day of Judgment because as Christ was, so am I in this world. (1 John 4:17)

34. I am more than a conqueror because of Him who loved me. (Romans 8:37)

35. I am crucified with Christ; nevertheless, I live by the faith of the Son of God, who loved me and gave Himself for me. (Galatians 2:20)

36. The pure water of the Word of God washes my body. (Hebrews 10:22)

37. I cast all of my care upon the Lord because He cares for me. (1 Peter 5:7)

38. I don't love the world or the things in the world because the love of the Father is in me. (1 John 2:15)

TUESDAY ACKNOWLEDGEMENTS

1. I am one with God. (John 17:22)

2. I am in Christ, and Christ is in the Father. (John 14:20)

3. I can do anything because I abide in Christ, and He abides in me. (John 15:5)

4. I am in Christ because I have been baptized into Christ. (Galatians 3:27-28)

5. Christ is in me, and He is my hope of glory. (Colossians 1:27)

6. I have the glory of God. (John 17:22)

7. I arise and shine because the glory of the Lord is risen upon me. (Isaiah 60:1)

8. God's glory is seen upon me. (Isaiah 60:2)

9. Gentiles come to my light and kings to the brightness of my rising. (Isaiah 60:3)

10. I shine like the brightness of the firmament because I am wise and turn many to righteousness. (Daniel 12:3)

11. My whole body is full of light because my eye is single. (Matthew 6:22; Luke 11:34)

12. I behold with an open face the glory of the Lord, and I am changed into the same image from glory to glory even as by the Spirit of the Lord. (2 Corinthians 3:18)

13. I am risen with Christ, and I seek those things that are above where Christ sits on the right hand of God. (Colossians 3:1)

14. I set my affections on things above and not on things on the earth because I am dead, and my life is hid with Christ in God; when Christ who is my life shall appear, then shall I also appear with Him in glory. (Colossians 3:2-4)

15. I am seated in Heavenly places in Christ Jesus. (Ephesians 2:6)

16. God provides for all of my needs because I seek first the Kingdom of God, and His righteousness. (Matthew 6:33)

17. I don't fear because I have the Kingdom, and it was my Father's good pleasure to give it to me. (Luke 12:32)

18. I reap a hundredfold of the Kingdom of God because I have a good heart that hears, understands, and stays committed to the Word of the Kingdom that is preached, and I don't let anything distract me from the Word of God that is sown in my heart. (Matthew 13:19-23; Mark 4:15-20)

19. I take the Kingdom of God by force. (Matthew 11:12)

20. I press into the Kingdom of God when I hear it preached. (Luke 16:16)

21. My eyes and ears are blessed because they see and hear things that many prophets and righteous men desired to hear and see but never saw or heard. (Matthew 13:16-17)

22. I am great in the Kingdom of God because I humble myself as a little child. (Matthew 18:1-4)

23. God exalts me because I humble myself. (Matthew 23:12)

24. God lifts me up because I humble myself in the sight of the Lord. (James 4:10)

25. God exalts me in due time because I humble myself under the Mighty Hand of God. (1 Peter 5:6)

26. I have been given all things that pertain to life and godliness through the knowledge of Him that called me to glory and virtue by His Divine power. (2 Peter 1:3)

27. I am a partaker of God's Divine nature through His exceeding great and precious promises, and I have escaped the corruption that is in the world through lust. (2 Peter 1:4)

28. I live because I mortify the deeds of my body through the Spirit. (Romans 8:13)

29. I inherit the promises of God because I have faith and patience. (Hebrew 6:12)

30. All the promises of God in Christ are yes and amen to me. (2 Corinthians 1:20)

31. There has not failed one good thing that the Lord spoke to me; all of it has come to pass. (Joshua 21:45)

32. Blessed be God who has given me rest according to all that He promised; there has not failed one Word of all His good promise which He promised me. (1 Kings 8:56)

33. The Words of Christ dwell in me richly in all wisdom. (Colossians 3:16)

34. God is my Father. (John 20:17; Matthew 6:10)

35. God is my Healer – Jehovah-Rapha. (Exodus 15:26)

36. God is my Provider – Jehovah-Jireh. (Genesis 22:10-14)

37. God is my Peace – Jehovah-Shalom. (Judges 6:24)

38. God is my Righteousness – Jehovah-Tsidkenu. (Jeremiah 33:16)

WEDNESDAY ACKNOWLEDGEMENTS

1. My body is a temple of the Holy Spirit. (1 Corinthians 3:16; 1 Corinthians 6:19; 2 Corinthians 6:16)

2. I have been sealed by the Holy Spirit of promise as a down payment before the Day of Redemption.
    (2 Corinthians 1:22; Ephesians 1:13; Ephesians 4:30)

3. The Holy Spirit leads me because I am a son of God.
    (Romans 8:14)

4. I am a king and priest unto God.
    (Revelation 1:6; Revelation 5:9-10)

5. I am a joint heir with Christ. (Galatians 3:29; Galatians 4:1-7)

6. I worship God in Spirit and in truth. (John 4:24)

7. I come boldly to the Throne of grace, obtain mercy, and I find grace to help me in my time of need. (Hebrews 4:16)

8. I have entered into the rest of God because I have believed the Gospel. (Hebrews 4:1-11)

9. I can do all things through Christ, which strengthens me.
    (Philippians 4:13)

10. The eyes of my understanding are opened, and I know the hope of my calling and what the riches of the glory of His inheritance is in the saints. (Ephesians 1:18)

11. The Kingdom of God is inside of me. (Luke 17:20-21)

12. I am a born-again son of God because I received and believed on the name of Jesus. (John 1:12; 1 John 3:1-3)

13. I am born again by the incorruptible Word of God, which lives and abides forever. (1 Peter 1:23)

14. I overcome the world because I am born of God, and my faith gives me the victory that overcomes the world. (1 John 5:4-5)

15. I have been born again by the Spirit of God. (John 3:6)

16. I am a son of God, and God sent the Spirit of His Son into my heart, crying Abba, Father. (Galatians 4:6)

17. I didn't receive the spirit of bondage again to fear, but I received the Spirit of adoption, whereby I cry, Abba, Father. (Romans 8:15)

18. I am no longer a servant but a son of God and an heir of God through Christ. (Galatians 4:7)

19. God does exceedingly abundantly above all that I ask or think, according to the power that works in me. (Ephesians 3:20)

20. I have an incorruptible inheritance that is undefiled and fadeth not away reserved in Heaven for me. (1 Peter 1:4)

21. I receive whatever I ask of the Father in the Name of Jesus. (John 15:16; John 16:23)

22. I boldly say the Lord is my helper, and I will not fear what man shall do to me because God has said that He will never leave me nor forsake me. (Hebrews 13:5-6)

23. Greater is He that is in me than he that is in the world. (1 John 4:4)

24. I am filled with all the fullness of God. (Ephesians 3:19)

25. God's Spirit is upon me, and God put His Words in my mouth, and they don't depart from my mouth because I am in Covenant with Him. (Isaiah 59:21)

26. I reap in due season because I don't faint. (Galatians 6:9)

27. I sow to the Spirit and reap Everlasting Life. (Galatians 6:8)

28. I don't grow weary in well doing. (Galatians 6:9)

29. I wait upon the Lord, and He renews my strength. (Isaiah 40:31)

30. I mount up with wings as eagles, I run, and I am not weary; I walk, and I don't faint. (Isaiah 40:31)

31. God satisfies my mouth with good things so that my youth is renewed like the eagles. (Psalm 103:5)

32. I enter into the Holy of Holies with boldness. (Hebrews 10:19-20)

33. I know the voice of Jesus and follow Him because He is my Shepherd. (John 10:4)

34. God directs my paths because I trust Him with all of my heart; I don't lean to my own understanding, and I acknowledge Him in all of my ways. (Proverbs 3:5-6)

35. I have life and peace because I am spiritually minded. (Romans 8:6)

36. I have the spirit of wisdom and revelation in the knowledge of Him. (Ephesians 1:17)

37. I have oil in my lamp, and I am ready for the return of my Bridegroom because I am one of five wise virgins, and I know Christ. (Matthew 25:1-13)

THURSDAY ACKNOWLEDGEMENTS

1. The truth of the Word of God sanctified me. (John 17:17)

2. I am sanctified and perfected forever. (Hebrews 10:14)

3. I am perfect even as my Father in Heaven is perfect. (Matthew 5:48)

4. My heart was cleansed from an evil conscience by the sprinkling of the blood of Jesus. (Hebrews 10:22)

5. I have a pure conscience. (1 Timothy 3:9)

6. I am holy even as God is Holy. (1 Peter 1:15-16)

7. I cannot sin because I am born of God, and His seed remains in me. (1 John 3:9)

8. If I sin, God is faithful and just to forgive my sins and cleanse me from all unrighteousness when I confess them. (1 John 1:9)

9. I don't sin because God's fear is before my face. (Exodus 20:20)

10. I am not wise in my own eyes, but I fear the Lord and depart from evil. (Proverbs 3:7)

11. The Laws of God are written on my heart and my mind. (Hebrews 10:16)

12. My sins and iniquities are remembered no more. (Hebrews 10:17)

13. As far as the east is from the west, God has removed my transgressions from me. (Psalm 103:12)

14. God has subdued my iniquities and cast all of my sins in the depths of the sea. (Micah 7:19)

15. The Law of the Spirit of life in Christ Jesus made me free from the law of sin and death. (Romans 8:2)

16. I am a disciple of Jesus because I continue in His Word, know the truth, and the truth makes me free. (John 8:31-32)

17. I am not a servant to sin because Jesus made me free. (John 8:34-36)

18. Sin does not have dominion over me because I am not under the law but under grace. (Romans 6:14)

19. I have no condemnation because I am in Christ, and I don't walk after the flesh, but I walk after the Spirit. (Romans 8:1)

20. I have the benefit of God forgiving all of my iniquities. (Psalm 103:3)

21. I have the benefit of God healing all of my diseases. (Psalm 103:3)

22. I have the benefit of God redeeming my life from destruction. (Psalm 103:4)

23. God crowns me with lovingkindness and tender mercies. (Psalm 103:4)

24. I am a new creation, because I am in Christ; old things are passed away, behold all things are become new. (2 Corinthians 5:17)

25. I speak to mountains with my faith, and they move. (Matthew 17:20; Matthew 21:19-22; Mark 11:21-23)

26. I have whatever I say because I believe the things I say shall come to pass. (Mark 11:23)

27. None of my words fall to the ground. (1 Samuel 3:19)

28. I have faith in God to speak to mountains and nothing is impossible to me. (Matthew 17:20)

29. All things are possible to me because I believe. (Mark 9:23)

30. I don't stagger at the promise of God through unbelief, but I am strong in faith, and I give glory to God. (Romans 4:20)

31. I walk by faith and not by sight. (2 Corinthians 5:7)

32. I am not fearful because I have faith. (Mark 4:40)

33. I please God with my faith because I believe that He is, and He rewards me because I diligently seek Him. (Hebrews 11:6)

34. I am not afraid because I only believe. (Mark 5:36)

35. I receive everything I ask for and desire in prayer because I believe I have received them. (Matthew 21:22; Mark 11:24)

36. Whatever I ask, I receive from God because I keep His commandments and do those things that are pleasing in His sight. (1 John 5:22)

37. I am a mature son of God, and I am no longer in bondage under the elements of the world. (Galatians 4:1-6)

38. Nothing is restrained from me, which I imagine to do. (Genesis 11:6)

FRIDAY ACKNOWLEDGEMENTS

1. In God, I live, move, and have my being. (Acts 17:28)

2. I have peace with God through my Lord Jesus Christ because I have been justified by faith. (Romans 5:1)

3. I abide in Christ, and His Words abide in me. (John 15:7)

4. I have a spirit of power, love, and a sound mind.
   (2 Timothy 1:7)

5. I have authority in Christ over all the power of the enemy, and nothing shall by any means hurt me. (Luke 10:19)

6. I never thirst because I have a well of water in me that springs up into Everlasting Life. (John 4:14)

7. The Holy Spirit flows out of my belly as a river of life.
   (John 7:37-38)

8. I have life in me because I eat the flesh of the Son of man and drink His blood. (John 6:53)

9. I dwell in the secret place of the Most High, and I abide under the shadow of the Almighty. (Psalm 91:1)

10. I will say of the Lord, He is my refuge and my fortress: my God; in Him will I trust. (Psalm 91:2)

11. God delivers me because I set my love upon Him.
    (Psalm 91:14)

12. God set me on high because I know His name. (Psalm 91:14)

13. I call upon God, and He answers me. (Psalm 91:15)

14. God is with me in trouble and delivers me and honors me.
    (Psalm 91:15)

15. God satisfies me with long life and shows me His salvation. (Psalm 91:16)

16. I have the same mind that was in Christ, who being in the form of God, thought it not robbery to be equal with God, and I take on the form of a servant being found in fashion as a man, and I humble myself and become obedient unto the death of the cross and God highly exalts me. (Philippians 2:5-6)

17. I am an overcomer and inherit all things, and God is my God, and I am His son. (Revelation 21:7)

18. I overcame the devil by the blood of the Lamb and the word of my testimony. (Revelation 12:11)

19. I overcame the spirit of the antichrist because greater is He that is in me than he that is in the world. (1 John 4:3-4)

20. God anointed me, and I know all things. (1 John 2:20)

21. I don't need anyone to teach me because the anointing abides in me and teaches me all things. (1 John 2:27)

22. Goodness and mercy follow me all the days of my life, and I will dwell in the house of the Lord forever. (Psalm 23:6)

23. No weapon formed against me shall prosper. (Isaiah 54:17)

24. Every tongue that rises up against me in judgment I condemn. (Isaiah 54:17)

25. Yeah, though I walk through the valley of the shadow of death, I fear no evil, for God is with me; His rod and staff comfort me. (Psalm 23:4)

26. I have life, and I have life more abundantly because of Jesus. (John 10:10)

27. I have the perfect peace of God because I keep my mind stayed on Him. (Isaiah 26:3)

28. I don't worry about anything, but in everything, by prayer and supplication with thanksgiving, I make my requests known to God, and the peace of God, which passes all understanding, keeps my heart and mind through Christ Jesus. (Philippians 4:6-7)

29. I remember the Lord my God and acknowledge that it is He who gives me the power to get wealth so that He may establish His Covenant, which He sware unto our fathers as it is this day. (Deuteronomy 8:18)

30. My God supplies all of my needs according to His riches in glory by Christ Jesus. (Philippians 4:19)

31. I prosper and I am in health even as my soul prospers. (3 John 1:2)

32. I walk uprightly, and God does not withhold any good thing from me. (Psalm 84:11)

33. I delight myself in the Lord, and He gives me the desires of my heart. (Psalm 37:4)

34. I prosper, and I am successful because I meditate in the Word of God day and night, and His Word does not depart out of my mouth. (Joshua 1:8)

35. The Lord is my God, and He teaches me to profit and leads me in the way I should go. (Isaiah 48:17)

36. The Lord is my Shepherd, and I shall not want. (Psalm 23:1)

37. I abide forever because I do the will of God. (1 John 2:17)

38. I am blessed in my deeds because when I hear the Word of God, I do it and continue in it, and I am not a forgetful hearer. (James 1:22-25)

SATURDAY ACKNOWLEDGEMENTS

1. God always causes me to triumph in Christ.
(2 Corinthians 2:24)

2. I am greater than John the Baptist because I am in the Kingdom of God. (Matthew 11:11)

3. No one can be against me because God is for me.
(Romans 8:31)

4. God, who spared not His own Son but delivered Him up for me, freely gives me all things with Christ. (Romans 8:32)

5. I have received the Spirit of God, and I know the things that are freely given to me by God. (1 Corinthians 1:12)

6. I have the mind of Christ. (1 Corinthians 2:16)

7. I am complete in Him, who is the Head of all principality and power. (Colossians 2:10)

8. The Holy Spirit guides me into all truth. (John 16:13)

9. The Holy Spirit shows me things to come. (John 16:13)

10. I have eternal life because I know God and Jesus Christ, whom He sent. (John 17:3)

11. I walk in the Spirit, and I don't fulfill the lust of the flesh. (Galatians 5:16)

12. I walk in the Spirit, because I live in the Spirit. (Galatians 5:25)

13. The words I speak are Spirit, and they are life. (John 6:63)

14. I speak the oracles of God. (1 Peter 4:11)

15. I speak the Words of God because God doesn't give me His Spirit by measure. (John 4:34)

16. The joy of the Lord is my strength. (Nehemiah 8:10)

17. I have faith in God. (Mark 11:22)

18. I walk in the newness of life. (Romans 6:4)

19. I take up my cross daily, deny myself, and follow Christ. (Matthew 16:24)

20. My house is built on a rock and survives any storm because I am wise by obeying all the Words of Christ. (Matthew 7:24-25)

21. My mortal body is quickened by the Spirit of Him that raised Jesus from the dead. (Romans 8:11)

22. By the stripes of Jesus, I was healed. (1 Peter 2:24)

23. I have been redeemed from the curse of the law because Jesus became a curse for me by hanging on a tree. (Galatians 3:13)

24. Through faith, I have the blessing of Abraham, which is the promise of the Spirit. (Galatians 3:14)

25. I am a citizen of Heaven. (Philippians 3:20)

26. I put on the Lord Jesus Christ and make no provision for the flesh. (Romans 13:14)

27. I put on the new man, which after God is created in righteousness and true holiness. (Ephesians 4:24)

28. I put on the new man which is renewed in knowledge after the image of Him that created him. (Colossians 3:10)

29. Jesus is with me. (Matthew 28:20)

30. I am in Christ who of God is made unto me wisdom, righteousness, sanctification and redemption. (1 Corinthians 1:30)

31. I have the nine fruits of the Spirit. (Galatians 5:22-23)

32. I operate in the gifts of the Spirit. (1 Corinthians 12:7-10)

33. I don't draw back, and I don't tempt God and limit the Holy One of Israel. (Psalm 78:41)

34. I am just and I live by faith, and God has pleasure in me because I don't draw back. (Hebrews 10:38)

35. I present my body as a living sacrifice, holy, acceptable unto God, which is my reasonable service. (Romans 12:1)

36. I am not conformed to this world, but I am transformed by the renewing of my mind. (Romans 12:2)

37. I prove what is the good and acceptable and perfect will of God. (Romans 12:2)

38. A thousand shall fall at my side and ten thousand at my right hand, but it shall not come nigh me, and only with my eyes shall I behold the reward of the wicked. (Psalm 91:7-8)

SUNDAY ACKNOWLEDGEMENTS

1. I am an ambassador for Christ. (2 Corinthians 5:20)

2. I am strong, and I do exploits because I know God. (Daniel 11:32)

3. I do greater works than Christ because He went to the Father, and I believe on Him. (John 14:12)

4. I don't get drunk with wine, but I am filled with the Holy Spirit. (Ephesians 5:18)

5. I speak the Word of God with boldness because I am filled with the Holy Spirit. (Acts 4:29-31)

6. I open my mouth and speak boldly to make known the mystery of the Gospel. (Ephesians 6:19-20)

7. The weapons of my warfare are not carnal but mighty through God to the pulling down of strongholds, casting down imaginations, and every high thing that exalts itself against the knowledge of God. (2 Corinthians 10:4-5)

8. I bring every thought captive into the obedience of Christ, and I revenge all disobedience because my obedience is fulfilled. (2 Corinthians 10:5-6)

9. I'm joined to the Lord, and I am one Spirit with Him. (1 Corinthians 6:17)

10. I am strong in the Lord and in the power of His might. (Ephesians 6:10)

11. I am bold as a lion because I am righteous. (Proverbs 28:1)

12. No evil shall befall me, neither shall any plague come near my dwelling, because I have made the Lord my refuge and habitation, and He gives His angels charge over me to keep me in all of my ways, and they bear me up in their hands lest I dash my foot against a stone. (Psalm 91:9-12)

13. I am not wise in my own eyes, but I fear the Lord and depart from evil. (Proverbs 3:7)

14. My days are prolonged because I fear the Lord. (Proverbs 10:27)

15. I have strong confidence because I fear the Lord. (Proverbs 14:26)

16. The secret of the Lord is with me because I fear Him, and He shows me His Covenant. (Psalm 25:14)

17. I withstand and stand in the evil day because I wear the whole armor of God. (Ephesians 6:13)

18. I stand with my loins girt about with truth, having on the breastplate of righteousness, my feet are shod with the preparation of the Gospel of peace, and I take the shield of faith and quench all of the fiery darts of the wicked one, and I put on the helmet of salvation, and I fight with the sword of the Spirit, which is the Word of God. (Ephesians 6:14-17)

19. God stretches out His hand to heal and does signs and wonders in the name of His Holy Child Jesus, because I am filled with the Holy Spirit, and I speak His Word with boldness. (Acts 4:29-31)

20. I preach the Gospel. (Mark 16:15)

21. Signs follow me. (Mark 16:17-18)

22. I cast out devils in the Name of Jesus. (Mark 16:17)

23. I speak with new tongues. (Mark 16:17)

24. I take up serpents. (Mark 16:18)

25. If I drink any deadly thing, it shall not hurt me. (Mark 16:18)

26. I lay hands on the sick, and they recover. (Mark 16:18)

27. I cleanse the lepers. (Matthew 10:8)

28. I raise the dead. (Matthew 10:8)

29. The Spirit of the Lord is upon me because He has anointed me to preach the Gospel to the poor. (Isaiah 60:1)

30. I go about doing good and healing all that are oppressed by the devil because God is with me and has anointed me with the Holy Spirit and power. (Acts 10:38)

31. I preach good tidings to the poor. (Luke 4:18)

32. I heal the brokenhearted. (Luke 4:18)

33. I proclaim liberty to the captives and set them free. (Isaiah 60:1)

34. I preach recovery of sight to the blind and open their eyes. (Luke 4:18)

35. I set at liberty them that are oppressed. (Luke 4:18)

36. I preach the acceptable year of the Lord. (Luke 4:18)

37. I am endued with power from on high because the promise of the Father came upon me. (Luke 24:49)

38. I have power because I was baptized in the Holy Spirit and speak in tongues. (Acts 1:8)

ACKNOWLEDGEMENTS ARE A POWERFUL WAY IN WHICH WE COME INTO AGREEMENT WITH WHO WE ARE AND WHAT WE HAVE IN CHRIST!

CHAPTER 12

FINAL REVELATIONS

O nce you are born again, you become a newly created *mature* son of God in the *Realm of the Spirit*. From this point forward, the goal of your Christian life is to renew your mind to the realities of your newly created mature spirit man. By obeying all of the Words of Christ, prayer, speaking in tongues, acknowledgements, putting on the New Man, receiving from anointed ministers, and adhering to what you read in the Word of God, your mind is renewed. When you become more Christ-like, you will experience the glories of the New Testament promises, as we have revealed in this book. Becoming more Christ-like through the renewing of your mind to the mind of Christ is what the Bible calls being *"spiritually minded."*

> **Romans 8:6 (KJV)**
> *6 For to be carnally minded is death; but to be **spiritually minded** is life and peace.*

You grow and become spiritually minded by desiring the pure milk of the Word of God until you can consume the meat of the Word of God.

The meat of the Word of God is consumed by a believer who has matured in their soul by hearing and living the Word of God. They can spiritually see and are living in the deeper truths of God. The profound truths from God's Word are only revealed to those ready to assume the responsibility that comes with the mysteries of God. Our duty as believers is to spiritually grow to a place where we consume the meat of the Word of God. When a believer doesn't grow past the milk of the Word, the Bible says they are *dull of hearing*, which is the same as being carnally minded.

> **Hebrews 5:11-14 (KJV)**
> *11 Of whom we have many things to say, and hard to be uttered, **seeing ye are dull of hearing.** 12 For when for the time ye ought to be teachers, ye have need that one teach you again which be the first principles of the oracles of God; **and are become such as have need of milk, and not of strong meat. 13 For every one that useth milk is unskilful in the word of righteousness: for he is a babe. 14 But strong meat belongeth to them that are of full age,** even those who by reason of use have their senses exercised to discern both good and evil.*

During His ministry, Jesus revealed when quoting from the Prophet Isaiah that people's hearts waxed gross, their ears were dull of hearing, and they closed their eyes.

> **Matthew 13:15 (KJV)**
> *15 For this people's heart is waxed gross, **and their ears are dull of hearing, and their eyes they have closed; lest at any time they should see with their eyes and hear with their***

ears, and should understand with their heart, and should be converted, and I should heal them.

According to the Bible, believers are babes in Christ when they walk in their carnal minds. The Apostle Paul told the Church at Corinth that he could only feed them with milk, not meat because they were babes in Christ. The word babe means: infant, immature, simple-minded, untaught, unskilled, and unlearned.

> **1 Corinthians 3:1-2 (KJV)**
> *1* **And I, brethren, could not speak unto you as unto spiritual, but as unto carnal, even as unto babes in Christ.**
> *2* **I have fed you with milk, and not with meat:** *for hitherto ye were not able to bear it, neither yet now are ye able.*

It is spiritually dangerous to live with a carnal mind. The Bible says the carnal mind is an enemy against God. The carnal mind is an enemy of God because it is connected to this world, which is connected to the devil. The carnal mind operates only in what it can see, hear, feel, and touch. The spiritual mind operates by seeing into the unseen *Realm of the Spirit* through the Word of God. It's not until you disconnect from this world and begin to see things from God's perspective by the power of the Holy Spirit that you are considered spiritual. This is called spiritual maturity in God's eyes.

> **Romans 8:5-8 (KJV)**
> *5 For they that are after the flesh do mind the things of the flesh; but they that are after the Spirit the things of the Spirit.*
> *6* **For to be carnally minded is death; but to be spiritually minded is life and peace.** *7* **Because the carnal mind is**

> **enmity against God:** *for it is not subject to the law of God, neither indeed can be. 8 So then they that are in the flesh cannot please God.*

Growing up spiritually in your soul and mind requires commitment, time, and effort. God never promised that growing up spiritually would be easy. The road to spiritual maturity, where your eyes are opened to the Realm of the Spirit, is not for the faint of heart. However, because it is a less traveled road with high demands, anyone who chooses this path will be well rewarded in this life and the future eternal life. Jesus said the Kingdom of God was likened to a man who found a treasure in a field, hid the treasure, and sold everything to buy that field. You have to be willing to go all in with God to grow up spiritually.

> **Matthew 13:44 (KJV)**
> **44 Again, the kingdom of heaven is like unto treasure hid in a field; the which when a man hath found, he hideth, and for joy thereof goeth and selleth all that he hath, and buyeth that field.**

SPIRITUAL EYES

The inward eyes of a mature believer are open to the *Realm of the Spirit,* because they are committed to their spiritual growth. Jesus said those who could see who He was and what He was teaching had blessed eyes. Their eyes were blessed because they saw in the *Spirit* things that many prophets and kings of the past desired to see and didn't see. Today, we can open our Bibles and behold the wonderous truths of the Gospel and who God created us to be because of what Jesus has done for us. But we have a greater responsibility because of the potential we now have in

God. We must take the Word of God and consume it until we spiritually grow up.

> *Luke 10:23-24 (KJV)*
> *23 And he turned him unto his disciples, and said privately,* ***Blessed are the eyes which see the things that ye see: 24 For I tell you, that many prophets and kings have desired to see those things which ye see, and have not seen them; and to hear those things which ye hear, and have not heard them.***

In the Book of Ephesians, the Apostle Paul prayed that the eyes of their understanding would be enlightened so that they might know the hope of His calling and the riches of the glory of His inheritance in the saints. Everything you are looking and hoping for has already been given to you in the *Realm of the Spirit*. You must **Open Your Eyes** to see it. Once you see into the *Realm of the Spirit* and it comes into clear focus through the eyes of your imagination, you can receive your inheritance by faith.

> *Ephesians 1:18-19 (KJV)*
> *18* ***The eyes of your understanding being enlightened; that ye may know what is the hope of his calling, and what the riches of the glory of his inheritance in the saints,*** *19 And what is the exceeding greatness of his power to us-ward who believe, according to the working of his mighty power,*

FAITH IN GOD

Faith is such a hot topic in the Bible because it is only by faith we can see into the *Realm of the Spirit* and please God. God is pleased when His children walk by faith and not by sight. Walking by faith means you have chosen not to live by your physical senses but by the Word of God. You believe the Word of God above your physical senses. You are not moved by what you see or hear but by what you believe. You *Open Your Eyes* by faith and see the invisible; as you see the invisible, the invisible becomes visible.

When a believer chooses to *Open Their Eyes* to the *Realm of the Spirit*, they will start seeing the power of God manifest in their life. The power of God only operates through the faith of a believer who can see what unbelievers can't see. Faith sees everything that God has already accomplished and is not trying to get God to do something He has already done through the finished work of Christ. Everything that pertains to life and godliness has already been given to us, and when we receive God's promises, we partake in His *Divine Nature*. Maturity takes place in our minds and souls as we manifest the Word of God since we are already mature in Christ in the *Realm of the Spirit.*

> ### 2 Peter 1:3-4 (KJV)
> *3 According as his divine power hath given unto us all things that pertain unto life and godliness, through the knowledge of him that hath called us to glory and virtue: 4 Whereby are given unto us exceeding great and precious promises: that by these ye might be partakers of the divine nature, having escaped the corruption that is in the world through lust.*

A big part of Biblical faith is *Opening Your Eyes* and discovering who you are and what you have in the *Realm of the Spirit.* All the Patriarchs in the Bible had faith, and that is why God was pleased with them. The

Eleventh Chapter of Hebrews is considered the **Great Hall of Faith** because these saints *Opened Their Eyes* and chose to believe God and His Word rather than what they saw with their natural eyes. They saw the invisible God with their faith (Hebrews 11:27) and all of His promises, which is why God was pleased with them.

> **Hebrews 11:6 (KJV)**
>
> *6 **But without faith it is impossible to please him:** for he that cometh to God must believe that he is, and that he is a rewarder of them that diligently seek him.*

When the Bible commands us to walk and live by faith, God directs us to live out of our spirit. When you begin living and walking in the Spirit, a paradigm shift occurs in your thinking. The Holy Spirit quickens your mind, and with your inward eyes of imagination, you see the glories of the unseen realm where all of the promises of God are waiting to be inherited. The Word of God teaches us that the unseen realm is eternal, and the seen realm is temporal.

> **2 Corinthians 4:18 (KJV)**
>
> *18 **While we look not at the things which are seen, but at the things which are not seen: for the things which are seen are temporal; but the things which are not seen are eternal.***

Jesus, the Author and Finisher of our faith, has blessed and chosen us to see into the unseen *Realm of the Spirit.* You begin to grasp your Heavenly potential when you realize the magnitude of your calling for your eyes to be opened in a way that humankind could never see before Christ came. By seeing into the *Realm of the Spirit* through the eyes of your faith-filled imagination, a whole new world of opportunity opens up to you.

There is unlimited potential in the *Realm of the Spirit*, which Jesus taught when He said nothing is impossible for those who believe. Jesus was living out of His Spirit and seeing miracles because He was not bound to the constraints of this physical world. When you read the Gospels, you discover that Jesus offered whoever would hear and obey His Words the opportunity to see and live in the *Realm of the Spirit* with Him. Religion reduces the Words of Christ to being a good person by operating in the seen realm, whereas Jesus taught His disciples to *Open Their Eyes* and operate out of the unseen realm.

Through the power of the Gospel message, God can take an unbeliever and change them from the inside out. As believers in Christ, there is no limit to what God can do through you if you *Open Your Eyes.* When you take the limits off God, you allow His power to work through you. The children of Israel limited God during the time of Moses because they didn't believe in God and what He wanted to do through them in taking the Promised Land.

> **Psalm 78:41 (KJV)**
> *41 Yea, they turned back and tempted God,* ***and limited the Holy One of Israel.***

DIVINE TAKEAWAY

It is your responsibility and mandate to *Open Your Eyes* through the Word of God, renew your mind, and allow God to show you who you are and what you have in the *Realm of the Spirit.* No one can stand before

God and say He held them back from seeing who they are in the *Realm of the Spirit.* Mind renewal and spiritual growth are as easy as picking up your Bible, believing, adhering to what you have read, and asking God to *Open Your Eyes.* We have to take responsibility for our walk with God. Jesus did all He will ever do for you at the cross of Calvary. The question is, *"What will you do with what He has done?"*

Your *Eyes Are Opened* to the Degree You:

- Read & study your Bible

- Obey *All* the Words of Christ

- Meditate on the Word of God

- Adhere to and speak the Word of God

- Pray without ceasing

- Speak in other tongues daily

- Use your imagination through the Power of God

- Acknowledge all Christ has done for you

- Put on Christ, the *new man* and the armor of God

- Be led by the Holy Spirit

- Receive from anointed ministers

- Renew your mind

When you *Open Your Eyes* and discover who you are in the *Realm of the Spirit,* you will not be ordinary. As a born-again son of God, the "*New You"* is unique, exceptional, powerful and outside the norm. Remarkable and astonishing manifestations of God's power are revealed through those who know who they are in Christ and what they have. You are a million times more powerful on the inside than on the outside, and you will accomplish more in your new life as a believer as you operate out of your spirit man than you ever could through your old man. What seems impossible to your old man is possible with your *New Man.*

God has privileged us in Christ to live above the ordinary human existence. As a born-again son of God filled with the Holy Spirit, you must choose to be extraordinary as you *Open Your Eyes* to all of the possibilities found in the *Realm of the Spirit.* God never intended for His people to be ordinary and powerless. The Holy Spirit takes it for granted that you are finished with your old man when you are born-again and believes you are ready to move into the *Realm of the Spirit.* As you live out of your newly created spirit, the Holy Spirit will reign supreme in your life, and you will experience all that God intended for you to inherit. The Holy Spirit will elevate you into the glories of the age to come as you taste and see all God has given and created you to be.

As we conclude this book, you must understand your *Divine Potential.* We have given you many keys in this book as a road map to empower you to *Open Your Eyes.* As you allow the Word of God to grow in your heart, there is no end to what God desires to reveal to you through your spiritual eyes. Once your *Eyes Are Opened*, it is impossible to overestimate the importance of the power of God working through the *New Man.* It is time to lift up your eyes, be passionate for God, and tap into a realm few believers experience. How can you remain the same when seeing who God made you to be in Christ and all you've been given? All you can do is *Open Your Eyes, Discover Who You Are in the Realm of Spirit,* and do the *IMPOSSIBLE!*

OPEN YOUR EYES AND SEE ON THE OUTSIDE WHAT YOU LOOK LIKE ON THE INSIDE!

ABOUT
VASYL PECHKO

Vasyl Pechko was born in a small village in Western Ukraine to his parents, Joseph and Mary. His father, Joseph, worked as a carpenter while pastoring a Church. Vasyl was raised as the firstborn son with four other siblings. During this time, Ukraine was still a part of the Soviet Union. When Vasyl was young, the communist regime of the Soviet Union persecuted Christians. This persecution, however, only strengthened Vasyl's dedication and faith in God.

At 17, God called Vasyl into ministry as a youth Pastor in his father's Church. Later, Vasyl became the Associate Pastor and worked in ministry alongside his father. In 1988, Vasyl married a beautiful young lady named Elina. Soon after they were married, God blessed them with two daughters born one year apart.

A few years later, Vasyl and his family, along with another missionary couple, had a revelation from the Lord that it was His will for them to plant a Church in a nearby town where there weren't any Christian Churches. When the Soviet Union collapsed, the Ukrainian people felt betrayed by the Communist Party. Because of this collapse, many Ukrainians sought the truth, which made them open to the Gospel. This Newly planted Church grew with many new converts to Christianity because of the downfall of Communism. Because of this growth, Vasyl, now the Senior Pastor, could plant new churches in nearby cities.

In 2003, Vasyl and his family moved to the United States and settled in Sacramento, California. In their first few years living in the United States, Vasyl and his wife Elina studied English and established themselves. In 2005, Vasyl began planting a Church for Ukrainians, and God blessed them with two boys. Then, in 2009, Vasyl was called to be the Bishop of an English-speaking Church called New Life Worship Center. Through weekly services, he has a local congregation and reaches other nations through his online media outreach. Brother Vasyl also hosts a TV program called Faith Secrets, where he interviews men and women of God.

2024 was challenging for Bishop Vasyl and his family as their firstborn daughter, Alina, went to be with the Lord at 34. Alina was a bright person who ministered to many people as an Optometrist. Alina was happily married to a young veteran named Andrew, but before she passed, she gave birth to a beautiful young daughter.

Brother Vasyl and his wife, Elina, have spent many hours in fellowship with Vince and his wife, Eunice. Their many hours spent together in the Presence of the Lord have brought their families closer together. Through their friendship, God has called them to write this book together as a legacy of their calling in God. Vasyl believes that everyone who opens their hearts and eyes through faith can see the treasure given to us in Christ. Vasyl & Elina strongly believe in God and His provision for everyone who believes.

INVITE VASYL TO SPEAK

VISIT

WWW.NLWCCOGOP.COM

ABOUT
VINCE BAKER

Vince Baker was born in Southern California and later lived on seventeen acres just north of Sacramento. As a child, Vince was raised as a Southern Baptist. Vince was always drawn to the Lord and even said he wanted to be a preacher at an early age.

Vince's life was uneventful until, one day, he encountered God while driving in his car at the age of 17. God manifested Himself to Vince so powerfully that his life would never be the same. After this experience, Vince became a Christian and dedicated his life to the Lord. In that same month, Vince received a book from his Christian Grandmother called "The Secret of His Power." This book was about a famous miracle-working Evangelist named Smith Wigglesworth. God used this book to prepare Vince for ministry.

Vince decided to attend a Christian high school in his senior year. At this school, Vince was introduced to a seasoned Evangelist who took local Churches to feed the poor and evangelize. Vince found out he lived near this Evangelist and started traveling with him. During this time, Vince became his right-hand man and saw many amazing miracles on the streets through this ministry. This ministry was called to train the Church on evangelizing with power. Vince traveled up and down the West Coast, ministering to the homeless and helpless while equipping the Church. To this day, Vince has a big heart for the poor, homeless, and hurting people.

Within a short time, Vince heard from God to attend Bible College. Through confirmation from God and a miracle of his tuition being paid in full, Vince started to study the Bible more deeply at this Bible College. Vince's foundational training from the Word of God during this time was priceless. Vince ended up graduating as a Valedictorian from this Bible College.

After Bible College, Vince started ministering to kids at a Christian school, taught Sunday School, and functioned in the local Church. Vince later moved into full-time ministry and was an assistant pastor at a local Church for five years during the mid-'90s'.

As the assistant Pastor, Vince visited a Church where the Prophet Kim Clement was ministering. Prophet Kim Clement pulled Vince out of the crowd and prophesied over him. In that prophecy, God told Vince that He would use him mightily and needed to prepare himself.

Vince later worked in the marketplace, where he is the CEO and part-owner of Agora Advantage. God called Vince to the marketplace, but Vince knew that he would be called back into full-time ministry later in life. Agora Advantage has been a fantastic position where Vince has grown in many ways. As a sign from God, Vince was voted in as the CEO of Agora Advantage on the Day of Pentecost.

As Vince neared the prophesied time that God would bring him back into full-time ministry, he began seeking the Lord more deeply. During this time, Vince had another unforgettable encounter with God regarding the Ark of the Covenant. God gave Vince a vision of four men carrying the Ark of the Covenant into a Church. The Holy Spirit spoke to Vince and said, "Wherever you read Ark of the Covenant in the Old Testament, think Holy Spirit. Wherever you read the Holy Spirit in the New Testament, think of the Ark of the Covenant. Put the two together, and you will know Me."

Vince studied these two subjects everywhere he could find them in the Bible, and the Lord gave him tremendous insight into understanding and knowing more deeply about the Holy Spirit.

God also revealed to Vince a prophetic way to study the Bible from this experience. Vince went on to spend years in the Word of God, studying different subjects of the Bible as the Holy Spirit led him. At the leading of the Holy Spirit, Vince researched every place a word or phrase was found from the Old and New Testaments. Vince has done over four hundred of these studies, some of which took months to complete. The revelations that came out of these studies were life changing. Vince wrote down all these teachings and revelations, which make up many of the truths he writes about in his books and the messages he preaches today. Vince discovered that when you study a subject everywhere it is located in the Bible, you can receive the full counsel of God on that subject. Vince also received many dreams and visitations from God during this time.

God prophetically brought Bishop Vasyl into his life, and Brother Vasyl heard from God to make Vince a part of his Pastoral staff at New Life Worship Center. Vince preaches the Word of God regularly with Bishop Vasyl. A deep friendship has been formed in their lives as they both recognize God's destined plan to bring them together.

Vince has a unique calling where he can preach, teach, prophecy, move in the gifts of the Spirit, bring healing, and perform miracles by the power of the Holy Spirit. Vince is called to help the body of Christ come into their destiny and High Calling.

Currently, Vince resides in Northern California with his wife, Eunice, and their two dogs, enjoying God's many blessings.

INVITE VINCE TO SPEAK

VISIT

WWW.VINCEBAKERMINISTRIES.COM

ADDITIONAL BOOK BY
<u>VINCE BAKER</u>

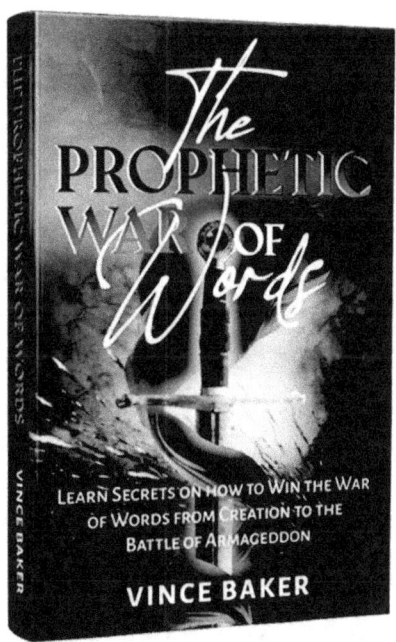

www.amazon.com/author/vincebaker
www.VinceBakerMinistries.com

ADDITIONAL BOOK BY
VINCE BAKER

www.amazon.com/author/vincebaker

www.VinceBakerMinistries.com

ADDITIONAL BOOK BY
<u>VINCE BAKER</u>

www.amazon.com/author/vincebaker
www.VinceBakerMinistries.com

ADDITIONAL BOOK BY
<u>VINCE BAKER</u>

www.amazon.com/author/vincebaker

www.VinceBakerMinistries.com

ADDITIONAL BOOK BY
<u>VINCE BAKER</u>

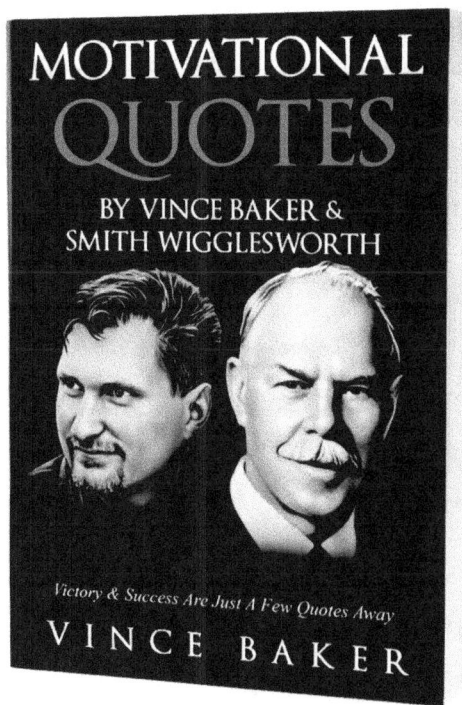

www.amazon.com/author/vincebaker

www.VinceBakerMinistries.com